# ON GUARDED

"As a lifeguard in the 1980s, I immediately recognized the life-and-death stakes and responsibilities. Debbie Friedman's detail transported me back to the beach—I could feel the tension of that huge rip and the rescues that followed. She celebrates the women who paved the way for all of us to guard California's beaches. Her own rise through the profession is a testament to passion and leadership. I didn't want the book to end."

**—Julie Moss**
Ironman Hall of Fame triathlete; speaker and author

"An immersive, unexpected account of a demanding profession where lives were on the line—shaped by the realities of swimming through surf to save lives."

**—Shannon Huffman Polson**
U.S. Army Apache helicopter pilot; author of *The Grit Factor*

"Debbie Friedman has created a unique and significant work with GUARDED. At once sobering, thoughtful, and amusing, the book tells the story of real people confronting barriers in what had long been an exclusively male enclave. Told without malice and grounded in lived experience, it is voiced through the personal stories of the pioneering women who stepped into the profession. And…it's a great read."

**—Mike Brousard**
California State Lifeguard; author

# *ON GUARDED*

"GUARDED is an incredible dive into the world of lifeguard-ing and the story of women forging a path into the field. Debbie Friedman deftly glides between her own experience as a trailblazer and those of other women, with evocative stories of saves so vivid you almost smell the sea air and feel the sand beneath your feet."

**—Dr. Diane Bridgeman**

"In an age of sensationalism, Debbie Friedman delivers the real dispatch from the trenches of early lifeguarding. GUARDED finally gives women their chapter in the renaissance of lifeguard culture—with a woman's authority. Fierce. Honest. Must-read."

**—Drasko Bogdanovic**
Founder, The Lifeguard Project

"Debbie Friedman's story proves that the drive to save a life is not about gender. Standards were met—and smashed."

**—Coral Kemp**
California Lifeguard and Champion Surf Lifesaving Competitor

# GUARDED
## WOMEN, WATER, AND SAVING LIVES

DEBBIE FRIEDMAN

TOWER ONE PRESS

Library of Congress Control Number: 2025927750

ISBN 979-8-9937664-0-9 (paperback)
ISBN 979-8-9937664-1-6 (e-book)

Jacket design and cover photograph © 2025 Kim Ferrell
Back cover photograph by Mike Brousard
Interior design by Amy Lynn Foster
Author photograph by Martina Nicholson

*For Kim Raymont-Webb*
*1959 – 2015*

## *Author's Note*

This book draws from my years as a lifeguard in California during the 1970s and '80s, woven together with the stories of other women lifeguards from the same era. It is built from memory, journals, and conversations. Some names and details have been changed. In places, I've recreated dialogue, timelines, and characters to capture what happened—and how it felt.

These are only a few stories among many, drawn from a time when life—especially on the beach— was understood in narrow terms. I have tried to write honestly about our experiences, and to leave room for many more voices to be heard.

# GUARDED

## WOMEN, WATER, AND SAVING LIVES

# Contents

# Queen Calafia's Guards

*Very close to the Garden of Eden, there*
*was said to be an island of gold, ruled*
*by strong and beautiful Black women.*
*This island was also populated by griffins—*
*mythical lion-eagle creatures that the women*
*kept as pets. Any man who found his way onto*
*this island was killed and fed to the beasts.*
*The name of this mythical island? California.*

**Queen Calafia was the ruler of**
**the Island of California.**

—from *The Exploits of Esplandian,*
Garci Ordóñez de Montalvo, 1510

The Spanish explorers of the 16th century were captivated by this legend. When they reached the West Coast, they named California after Queen Calafia, imagining it as a paradise of wild beauty and untamed freedom ruled by fierce women.

In the myth, Queen Calafia and her warriors were fearless. They hunted with griffins, patrolled their golden shores, and ruled over an unspoiled land of bounty. But as I imagined it, the queen grew restless. One day she and her warriors sailed away on warm winds and following seas, leaving behind only her name and her legend.

Generations passed, and the Island of California became a paradise for men to claim. By the 20th century, Queen Calafia and her fierce protectors had been forgotten, replaced by men in red swim trunks and mirrored sunglasses who patrolled the beaches as if they had always belonged to them.

It wasn't until the 1970s that a handful of women challenged this story. Like Calafia's warriors, we were strong, skilled, and fearless. We claimed our place on California's beaches, standing guard over the waters that had always been ours. We were Queen Calafia's guards, protectors of the ocean, reclaiming our legacy.

1

## *Calafia Street*

"Rescue, Tower 3, one victim, straight out."

I left the phone off the hook, grabbed my bright-red rescue tube and fins, and climbed down the splintered ladder. My eyes locked on the struggling swimmer, thrashing against the pull of the rip current. I hit the sand running.

*Don't trip*, I told myself as I navigated sunbathers, umbrellas, and beach towels. The people I passed, trying not to kick sand on their towels or knock over their drinks, were oblivious that I was running to save a life.

It was August 1978 on San Clemente State Beach, and the water was 70 degrees—not quite tropical, but warm enough not to feel cold. A south swell had brought three-to five-foot waves with an outgoing tide, creating prime rescue conditions. I'd already made four rescues in that same rip current. Now another swimmer was in trouble.

*Another Marine.*

The Calafia Street parking lot sat behind my tower, and all the lifeguards knew: if you were a Marine from Camp Pendleton, just a few miles south, Tower 3 was your beach. This young Marine, my victim, had arrived on the beach with buzz-cut hair, pale skin, and no body fat. He wore the unofficial uniform—T-shirt and cut-off jeans, frayed and uneven. Most of our rescues at Tower 3 were Marines. They were young, fearless, and fit. For many it was their first time in the Pacific Ocean. Not every Marine needed saving, but every Marine was a potential rescue.

He was alone and tossed his towel down next to my tower without a glance in my direction. Like a magician, he grabbed the bottom of his T-shirt and swept both arms to the sky, his shirt flying off in one motion, revealing a bare pink chest. He looked to heaven, spread his arms wide, and sprinted full speed into the surf. I smiled. He was an image of unrestrained joy, laughing with no buddies watching.

Until the whitewater from an outside wave knocked him to his knees. He turned onto his back and floated, drifting into an inshore hole—a sudden drop-off that took him from knee-deep water to chest-deep in a step. When he tried to stand, the deeper water funneled him into a rip current—a powerful channel where the incoming surf returns seaward, like a fast-moving river flowing the wrong way. For this Marine, it was the wrong direction, pulling him beyond the surf zone, away from shore.

I tore off my T-shirt, down to my suit, and placed my hand on the rescue tube, a subtle signal to adjacent guards that I was watching a possible rescue.

My Marine turned around and tried to swim back toward shore. But instead of swimming horizontally, flat on the ocean's surface, his legs and hips sank. Suddenly he was vertical in the water, each exhausting stroke pulling him up and down, with zero progress toward shore. He clawed at the water with his elbows, fighting the current. Lifeguards called this "climbing the ladder."

I ran to the water, my heartbeat quickened. I calculated my entry point: fifty yards downcoast, so the upcoast current would push me toward him instead of pulling me away. Water rescues weren't an exact science. They were more like an art—a mix of training, instinct, and luck. Mistiming my entry or approach could mean the difference between life and death. No two rescues were ever the same, and assuming that one would be easy is a mistake that could cost a life.

I high stepped into the water. When I could no longer run, I dove under a wave and rolled into a ball to pull my fins onto my feet. With each kick, I propelled myself closer to him. With every stroke, I grabbed as much water as possible, pulling myself forward until I could see the panic on his face.

"You're okay," I said with confidence. "Turn around and grab the tube."

Like most obedient young Marines, he followed my instructions. I clipped the tube around his torso, told him to stay on his back, and swam us parallel to shore, out of the dirty, sandy current that had pulled him outside the surf. Backstroking us toward the beach, I used the incoming swells to speed up the return to shore.

When we reached standing-depth water, the Marine stood tall with newfound bravado.

"Let me go!" he yelled as a wave knocked us both down, and he hit the sandy bottom hard. I landed on top of him like he was a boogie board.

Lifeguard training taught me to protect myself first when making a rescue, just as flight attendants teach us to put on our oxygen masks first so we can help others. I'd never had to do that on an airplane, but back in the water, my Marine surfaced spitting salt water, his shorts askew over his butt. This time he followed my orders and gripped the tube tightly until we reached dry sand.

I spoke gently, not wanting to embarrass him.

"You can let go of the tube now." He stood with his head low, his shoulders hunched forward. I tried not to humiliate him further as I gave him my standard talk about rip currents and safe swimming places.

"What's your name?" I asked for my tally.

"Tom," he said, still dazed. "From Mt. Hood, Oregon."

I climbed back into my tower, hung up the phone's black handle, scanned my water, and replaced my tube so it was visible to the adjacent lifeguard towers.

Every summer, lifeguards along the California coast made rescues like this thousands of times. But in 1978, this rescue was unusual because it was made by me, one of the first women lifeguards in California.

Lifeguarding at its core, even all these decades later, remains very much the same as it was in its early years. There's better gear and training, but look up at any lifeguard in a tower, and you'll see a rescue tube, a pair of fins, and a guard ready to swim out and pull someone in trouble out of the surf and safely to shore.

But—and it's a big but—when the lifeguard is a woman, that's not what the vast majority of people see.

What they really see is *Baywatch*.

In 1989, the TV series introduced lifeguarding to an international audience in more than 100 countries. C.J. Parker, portrayed by Pamela Anderson, was the first woman lifeguard many people had ever seen. Even today, when I mention I was a lifeguard, the most common response is: "Like *Baywatch*, right?"

Women guards, past and present, collectively roll our eyes as we reconcile the realities of our job with the enduring image that *Baywatch* projected to its 1.1 billion viewers: Pamela Anderson, styled long blond hair, heaving breasts, running in slow motion down the beach.

My early mentors and friends wrote books filled with lifeguard tales—stories of heroism, tragedy, and adventures. Lifeguard junkies, myself included, read them over and over, smiling, laughing, and crying through every chapter. Their stories inspired me to write this book—untold stories of the first generation of women who lined up on the beach, raced for a job, trained, and worked alongside men as California ocean lifeguards.

The first women hired at the beaches up and down the coast brought many unknowns. Lifeguards had always been men, primarily white men. Some of their concerns seem trivial now. Where would these "girl lifeguards" go pee? The men were nervous about the mysteries of menstruation—some even thought that a woman on her period in the water would attract sharks. And men guards spent way too much time and energy worrying about where we would go to the bathroom and change our clothes.

However, some concerns were more serious. "Are these females strong enough? Will our standards be compromised?" were common questions raised by the males who decided whether or not to hire a woman lifeguard.

It's been over 50 years since the City of Del Mar hired professional surfer Joyce Hoffman as a lifeguard in 1971. Now we have answers to many of those early questions.

We all figured out how to go to the bathroom and change our clothes. Strength remains relevant because lifeguarding has always been a highly physical job. Women have consistently met and exceeded the standards, past and present. Women have worked in all aspects of beach operations for decades, including training, supervision, and management. Obstacles, triumphs, and life-changing events marked our path.

As I sat down to write my thoughts about being a woman lifeguard, I dove headfirst into memories from more than

30 years ago. Names, photos, stories—the memories came rushing back.

Lifeguarding triggered my brain. I'd wake at night with an awful smell—the memory of falling into a hole with a dead sea lion. Walking on the beach below my house with my dog, Bernie, I closed my eyes. The salty air smelled and felt exactly the same way on my skin as it did when I was 18, standing in my lifeguard tower. As I shopped and went about business in town, I wondered if any of the young men I'd shared my life with on the beach had grown to look like the old guy in front of me at the market squeezing the avocados.

I became a lifeguard during times of fear and uncertainty as women crossed a red line in the sand to work with men. We each brought individual strengths, vulnerabilities, and reasons for wanting the job. Most of our stories had nothing to do with our gender but instead showed how lifeguarding changed us during our most formative years.

This was my life—raw, physical, terrifying, beautiful—and I know it wasn't just mine.

I've lived through 65 summers, and I spent 12 of them as a lifeguard. Why is so much of who I am rooted in those dozen years?

Joyce Hoffman, City of Del Mar, 1971

2

## *Joyce*

In Waterman's Plaza at Dana Point, on California Pacific Highway across from Doheny State Beach, Joyce Hoffman stands cast in bronze, immortalized among California's surf legends. Flanked by Hobie Alter, Phil Edwards, Bruce Brown, and John Severson, she is the lone woman in this pantheon of surf culture giants. Her plaque proclaims her as "The Best Woman Surfer in the World," a title she earned by dominating competitions and winning surf contests worldwide.

And tucked away on the plaque and among the gazillion things written about Joyce's life and career is a rarely mentioned title: California's First Female Ocean Lifeguard.

For two summers, starting in 1971, Joyce worked as a City of Del Mar Ocean Lifeguard. She stood for her team picture with 15 men to document the summer crew. With no official uniform for a woman, she wore a red bikini. Del Mar Lifeguard Captain Gardner Stevens' wife, Peggy, took Joyce's swimsuit home, sat at her kitchen table, and stitch by stitch, sewed the official lifeguard patch on the butt side of the bikini bottom, the only place it fit.

Joyce watched her water, swam into the surf to save people's lives, bandaged cut body parts, and sprinted down the beach to show visitors the safest spots to swim. When lost children cried, she held their hands and helped reunite them with their families. Then, after two summers, Joyce was gone, off to race motocross. Lifeguarding was another chapter in her extraordinary life, a small episode between surfing fame and her next adventure.

When she said yes to lifeguarding in 1971, at 23, she had already lived a life of accomplishment and celebrity. Joyce was the first woman to surf the legendary Banzai Pipeline, in Hawai'i. In 1963 the renowned photographer and filmmaker Bud Browne set up his camera on the North Shore of O'ahu. He kept his hands and camera steady as he filmed Joyce surfing as the thick wall of water pitched over her head. She became invisible on her board, tucked in the tube of water, with the shallow, clear, sharp reef below her. Spectators held their breath, waiting for her reappearance, and clapped with relief as she was spit out of the barrel. Browne called the Pipeline "one of the most dangerous surf spots in the world." Joyce was 16 years old.

As her fame grew, surfers walked into shops and found surfboards shaped by Phil Edwards featuring the Joyce Hoffman model for sale. *Surfing Magazine* planted Joyce's huge smile and sun-bleached blond hair on its glossy cover. *Life, Seventeen,* the *Los Angeles Times,* and *Sports Illustrated* ran articles about her. "Joyce was everywhere," wrote the *Dana Point Times.*

In the 1960s, surfing was a male tribe. Women surfers like Joyce started their own surfing league, creating space for themselves at surf contests, including the U.S. Championship and the Makaha International. Joyce trained six hours a day, swimming, running, and paddling, to compete at the highest levels of the surfing world, laying the groundwork for women's professional surfing.

Still dominating the surfing world at 23, Joyce caught the attention of another all-male tribe. Two lifeguards stroked their chins and, for a moment, thought wild and crazy thoughts outside the realm of rescues-as-usual.

Lifeguard lore has it that Huntington Beach Chief Vince Moorhouse sat down and talked with his pal, Del Mar Captain Gardner Stevens, about the possibility of Joyce working as a beach lifeguard. It was a radical idea—revolutionary—especially for two men with traditional leadership roles in guarding. I can picture them now, exchanging glances over this deviant idea, a woman guard—Joyce Hoffman.

They had watched Joyce win the U.S. Surfing Championships at the Huntington Beach Pier. She'd paddled out in front of them and launched herself into the biggest waves, carving back and forth on her board, leaving a clean whitewater trail behind on the face of her waves. At the end of each ride, she turned her board around and paddled back outside to surf more waves, over and over again.

The observing men, both with military backgrounds, square shoulders, and straight backs, had led the way as lifeguard programs expanded and were modernized in the 1950s and 1960s. By the time I started guarding, in the late 1970s, these men were considered old-school, lining up their staff to stand tall and stiff, military-inspection style. Khakis were the uniform of the day until the men stripped down to swim gear. I had a hard time imagining the chief of any department in those early lifeguard years taking off his uniform, even for a bath.

Moorhouse and Stevens weren't interested in including women in lifeguarding. They didn't see Joyce as a model for equality. Lifeguarding was a man's world. They believed that the work took men of courage and great strength to swim out into the ocean and rescue a person from the grip of death. The women they knew taught school, worked as secretaries, birthed their kids, and cooked their meals.

Joyce was an anomaly, a curiosity among men. If she could pass the lifeguard tryout test, it wouldn't mean other women could do the job. It would simply mean Joyce could. Moorhouse and Stevens decided to experiment and proposed the idea to Joyce. She said yes.


More than 50 years later, Joyce, now in her 70s, lives in Dana Point and still surfs. It was easy for me to find her phone number.

"Hello," she answered. Although I'm typically confident, I lost track of my purpose for calling her. The Pipeline raged through my brain, with pictures of Joyce standing in a tower with her strong surfing body, holding binoculars, looking out at the water. I was surprised to find myself starstruck.

After a quick reboot, I asked about her work on the beach. She laughed. "Lifeguarding wasn't on my radar, but I was asked to try out, so I thought, why not?"

On a cold spring morning in 1971, Joyce stood on Del Mar Beach for her lifeguard tryout swim. Surrounded by younger, less experienced male competitors, she was older, wiser, and had more ocean chops than every competitor alongside her. Most of the young men were just learning to shave, maybe sprouting a few chest hairs. Standing next to Joyce Hoffman, any of them would have had good reason to feel intimidated.

The press got word of Joyce's attempt to become a lifeguard, and as she prepared to swim, reporters shoved microphones at her and cameras clicked, ready to document the show.

"I felt a whole lot of womanhood pressure," she told me. *Where are the other women? Why am I the only one here?* Joyce asked herself.

I asked myself the same question years later while waiting for the starting gun to fire to compete for my chance to be a lifeguard.

Joyce shivered on the beach with her feet in the cold sand as she looked for the buoy marker beyond the surf line. A northwest swell brought in choppy, messy six-to eight-foot surf that crashed hard against the shore. Joyce wore her Hawaiian-print bikini, which she usually did when surfing and competing in warm tropical waters. In the 1970s, wetsuits were neither good quality nor allowed for swimming.

The ocean temperature hovered in the 50s, cold enough to cause hypothermia in anyone inexperienced in cold water. As she told me her story, I remembered my own cold-water swims. The first pain always landed deep in my head, like an ice cream headache on steroids. The cold squeezed my skull and kicked in a survival instinct to turn around and head straight for shore. My breathing became short and panicked, my lungs unable to fully expand. Blood rushed to protect my core and left my hands and feet numb. Despite every warning signal to stop, I moved forward through the surf, hoping my body could endure the pain and the reckless belief that it would subside.

I imagined what it felt like to be in Joyce's bare feet as she waited to swim. In that moment, her fame and surf titles meant nothing. Every move she made was evaluated and critiqued. Her performance would set the stage for future women who might try to cross into the lifeguard world of men:

"If the great Joyce Hoffman couldn't cut it…"

The starting gun fired, and the group sprinted to the water. The first big set of waves moved toward shore, and Joyce dove under the face of a wave, like a duck dive on her surfboard. She popped out the back and continued her momentum forward.

Some of the men behind her misjudged the surf. Panicking, they tried to swim up and over the faces of the waves. Joyce glanced back and saw the shadows of their bodies lifted into the back of the wave. She needed to keep swimming but knew what was next for the men caught inside. The lip curled, and in the next instant, they were pitched over the falls and slammed into the ocean bottom below. On the shore, spectators groaned in unison, "Ooooh, noooo."

Joyce continued to navigate the turbulent inside surf and lined up her strokes with the swim marker outside. Her years of surf training paid off as she powered through the water. She made a U-turn at the buoy, looked to shore, and increased her speed, taking advantage of incoming swells and breaking waves. Back on the beach, she finished with the leaders.

I imagined Captain Stevens nodding, wondering if Joyce might just be that special woman who could work alongside courageous and heroic lifeguard men.

But the swim was never enough. I can still hear the statement echoing across agencies along the coast as the first women lifeguards made it through the early qualifying tests:

"We still need to see if she can pass training and cut it on the beach."

Joyce did.

By the Fourth of July in 1971, Joyce was anointed one of the guys—a City of Del Mar Beach Lifeguard. She passed the same tryouts, completed the same training, and worked in the same capacity as her male colleagues. Joyce was recognized as California's first female ocean lifeguard.

I asked Joyce, as the first woman to guard Del Mar, if any men made her job difficult. Her answer came fast and firm.

"None of the guys would *dare* give me any guff," she said. "I knew I had more ocean credentials than anyone on the squad."

It was the only time I've heard a lifeguard, man or woman, no matter how many years working on the beach, project that kind of unshakeable confidence.

Part of Joyce's story was remarkably similar to my own, but other parts were very different.

Seven years after Joyce's tryout, I lined up with 100 men and no other women to swim for my job as an ocean lifeguard. Like Joyce, I brought physical strength to the job. But, unlike her, I also carried bags of insecurities and a lack of ocean knowledge. I was a pool swimmer, a stranger to salt water. At the age of 18, I was still self-conscious about how other people saw me. What's more, I had never seen a dead body, and the talk of death scared me. Beneath the strong physicality of my body, my emotions were still raw and close to the surface.

Between Joyce's summer as "The First Female Ocean Lifeguard" in 1971 and my own title as the first woman guard at San Clemente State Beach, about a dozen women were hired and named "The First Woman Lifeguard" on beaches along the coast of California where no women had worked before.

Firsts are rarely as clear-cut as written or proclaimed. Sally Ride, one of my heroes, was known as the first American woman in space in 1983. But decades earlier, in 1963, Valentina Tereshkova had orbited the earth as the first woman in space for the Soviet Union. Even with this knowledge, the United States refused to consider women for NASA.

The same held true for lifeguarding. Joyce's work as a lifeguard was an important achievement, but it didn't open the door for the rest of us. Up and down the coast, beach agencies operated under their own rules. That included when, or if, to hire women to guard their beaches.

The guards at Huntington City wore khaki uniforms, while on the other side of Beach Boulevard, Huntington State guards wore white T-shirts and blue gas-station-attendant pants. Most agencies still stripped down to reds to make rescues. State beaches used orange Duck Feet fins and Peterson rescue tubes. Los Angeles County guards carried red, hard, Burnside buoys, and fins were optional. Towers came in different colors, shapes, and sizes. Ranks and titles for lifeguards were all over the place. "Chief" meant you were in charge, but so did "Captain" or "Supervisor." Whatever the title, the lifeguard who ran the show put forth the agency's operating standards, budget, and vision.

The lifeguard in charge also decided whether or not to hire women. Joyce Hoffman's success as a lifeguard at Del Mar was not part of the discussion, as the men in charge sat in their lifeguard headquarters overlooking their stretch of ocean up and down the California coast and held court over whether a woman could "cut it here." Each head honcho believed their beach had the biggest surf and the gnarliest conditions. Even Joyce would have had to prove her mettle again if she wanted to work for a different beach.

In 1975, California State Parks trained its first three women, Kim Kiser, Cecilia (CeCi) Smith, and Sally Tuttle, to become ocean lifeguards. The agency employed about 600 seasonal lifeguards to work close to 300 miles of State Park coastline, making it the largest lifeguard agency in California. To ensure consistency in training and standards, all state park lifeguards received the same training at Huntington State Beach.

Kim and CeCi went through the Easter week training session and passed rookie school. They were both on the hiring list to work the San Diego Coast State Beaches. But Bob Isenor, the Aquatic Specialist for Southern California and the founding father of State Park lifeguarding, shut it down. As the story goes, he said, "No, they can't go. They are not strong enough."

With a flick of Isenor's wrist, Kim and CeCi were sent to Lake Perris, an urban, smoggy lake an hour inland.

Sally Tuttle went through training later that spring. She swam, ran, practiced rescues, and tested for a week. After she passed training, she arrived to work at Point Mugu and Ventura State Beaches. The men in charge north of the Los Angeles County line hired the new male graduates without questions, but debated Sally's virtues and qualifications. As they sized her up, Sally, who stood 6-foot-1, towered over the men in authority.

"They said they were unsure what to do with me," Sally told me almost 50 years later. "They considered making me do 10 pull-ups, and it was clear none of them could pass their own test."

After fretting and hand-wringing, the guards in charge relented and allowed Sally, a nationally ranked swimmer and graduate of lifeguard training, to be hired on their beach, with the biggest surf and gnarliest conditions.

The following year, Kim transferred to San Diego with little fanfare. CeCi stayed and enjoyed working at Lake Perris. And Sally started her second year as a Ventura lifeguard.

Beaches came in different sizes, shapes, and colors—some with big surf and heavy rescues, others packed with crowds that meant more prevention and dry-land action. Each agency had its own rules, leaders, and biases about hiring women. Some welcomed us, others didn't, and a few treated us like aliens who'd landed on their sand. Every woman hired became a first; the title was just an easy label.

Still, in Waterman's Plaza stands the statue of Joyce Hoffman, its plaque offering a quiet nod to her time as the first woman lifeguard in 1971.

3

## *My Path to Guarding*

*Gardena*

My brothers and I squirmed in the back seat of the powder-blue Ford Fairlane and established our territories.

"Move over," I ordered when I felt a hand or butt move past my imaginary boundary line.

It was summertime 1968, and I was 8 years old. This was our second trip of the summer to Redondo Beach, a 20-minute escape from Gardena in the South Bay of Los Angeles. My dad didn't want to pay for parking, so he circled the neighborhood until he found a free spot several blocks from the beach.

Once parked, my mom pulled out her compact mirror and gave herself a quick once-over, including a fresh coat of lipstick. My brothers and I each grabbed flowered bathroom towels we had brought from our house and slung them over our shoulders. Diving into the trunk of the car we fished out paper bags holding our lunches of bologna-and-cheese sandwiches and oranges—packed just like our school lunches. My dad heaved the large, blue canvas inflatable surf mat under one arm. In his other hand, he clutched his wallet and car keys while awkwardly managing a cigarette dangling from his mouth. I looked carefully to see if the ash would end up burning his lip.

Wearing only my swimsuit, I walked in the middle of the family. My eyes were wide open and straight ahead for the first glimpse of the ocean so I could shout, "I see the sea!" My brothers ran ahead, dragging their towels behind them, while my mom brought up the rear. She wore a white dress covered in big yellow and blue flowers and held her shiny black purse politely by its two short handles. I stared at her and wondered if she'd brought her swimsuit.

Bobby's sandwich fell out of his bag as he dragged his towel on the dirty sidewalk. Steven laughed at him. My dad's cigarette fell to the ground, and he muttered, shaking his head, as he headed back to the car for another pack of Marlboros. My brothers took over carrying the mat, pulling it behind them on the ground as we neared the beach. In all the commotion, I forgot to announce I'd seen the ocean first. But it was there, waiting for us.

My parents led the way onto the beach, and we followed, not quite sure where to put our things. My dad pointed to a spot in the sand, where we threw our towels and lunches into a pile. I moved quietly, grabbed the surf mat and announced,

"I'm the oldest. I go first."

"No way, that's not fair!" My brothers stomped their feet, but I ignored them and marched toward the waves.

I waded in, turned around as the whitewater approached, and launched myself onto the mat and into the wave, screaming and happy. The saltwater splashed against my face and into my mouth. I licked my lips and remembered how much I liked the taste of the ocean.

Nothing was better than bouncing up and down in the surf toward shore. I heard my brothers yell, "It's my turn!" I looked out at the water, ignored them, and headed back into the surf.

The ocean was pure freedom. There were no rules; no one yelled at me or told me what I could and couldn't do. The water made me feel like I could do anything, and I wanted to feel this way forever.

We managed these beach days only about twice each summer. When we got home, tar blotches stuck to the soles of my feet—a ritual part of a beach day in my mind. I stayed barefoot to avoid getting tar on my "slippers"—sandals in my neighborhood. Before I could enter the house, my mom gave me a rag and a chunk of butter to scrub off the tar, and once I showed proof of pink skin on the bottom of my feet, she opened the screen door and said, "You can come in now."

In the 1960s and 1970s, this part of Los Angeles was known for oil drilling; I saw "bird pumps" nodding up and down, over and over, every time we drove on the freeway.

The sky in Gardena was a haze of yellow and brown air. My dad smoked in the car with the windows rolled up, and when my brothers and I complained, he sputtered, "Stop your kvetching. Quit whining." Taking his right hand off the steering wheel, he'd make swatting motions at the three of us in the back seat.

Kids like me coughed our way through childhoods, filled with smog-choked skies and poor air quality. After dinner, I Love Lucy played on the living-room television while I curled up in bed reading a Nancy Drew mystery. Some nights, when my coughing didn't stop, my mom walked into my room and plugged in the humidifier. She took the book off my chest, opened the Vicks VapoRub, and massaged it into my chest until the coughing slowed, and I drifted to sleep. The smell of menthol still comforts me.

Beyond the summer beach trips and Sunday visits to see my grannie and granda in Costa Mesa, my bike took me everywhere else. It was pink and white, with a banana seat and pink sparkle tassels hanging from the handlebars. Helmets weren't a thing, but I always locked my bike because even in those "good old days," people stole bikes.

My best friend and next-door neighbor, Kathy Tanaka, and I were inseparable. We bought coils of red string licorice at the snack shack and sat on the equipment shed and watched my brothers play Little League baseball. I felt a strange frustration bubbling in my stomach. I wanted to be on the baseball field and feel the crack of the bat as I hit the ball into the outfield. I wanted to steal a base like my favorite Dodger, Maury Wills.

*Why can't I play Little League?* I wondered. *Am I a bad girl to want these things?* It was the kind of thought that made me glance around just to see if anyone else could tell what I was thinking. I never said it out loud.

I was the oldest child, the sister in charge, yet as I watched my brothers play baseball, I felt my status was fake. I wasn't allowed to play on the field. I sat with Kathy and laughed during these games, but I thought about what I wasn't allowed to do or become because I was a girl.

By the time I was 12, my world had expanded slightly, and I had two passions. One was dancing in the hallways of Curtis Junior High School. During lunch hours, the teachers let us play music. Like the hit television show *Soul Train*, we formed two lines of students between the walls of lockers. The record player would start spinning Motown, and we sang along with The Jackson 5's *ABC* and danced down the middle of the lines, showing off our best funky moves. When it was my turn, I danced without inhibition, proudly strutting and jiving through the train as my classmates laughed and clapped. In those moments, I wasn't just a little white girl; I was "The Greatest," just like Muhammad Ali.

I wore the best fashion of the day: Sears plaid bell-bottoms, wide belt, chunky shoes. My long blond hair fell halfway down my back; I was determined to grow it until it touched my pants. The school gave awards like Best Dancer, Biggest Afros, Longest Hair, and Cutest Couple. Although I was small and undeveloped in junior high, I was accepted because

I loved to dance. To this day, Stevie Wonder makes me jump out of my seat and get my groove on.

My other love was the Victoria Park swimming pool, next to the Goodyear Blimp Station across the Dominguez Channel. I rode my banana-seat bike there and spent whole summer days swimming. There was no swim team, but I kept myself entertained. I practiced the Australian crawl and sidestroke, which my mom learned as a child while swimming in Ireland. I liked holding my breath, going underwater, opening my eyes, and practicing the frog kick.

"Bump Butts" was a good trick. I found someone willing to hold hands with me and say, "Face me and lean backward. We'll push our feet together really hard."

If we timed it right, our butts met as we flipped into a backward somersault. I almost always came up with water in my nose and hair all over my face. It was a feat of pride and a small amount of shame. It felt nasty—like sex if I knew what sex was—the thought of butts touching. Remember, my mom was from Ireland.

Three lifeguard stands were spread out around the square pool. The guards wore white T-shirts with a big red cross on the front. They had whistles and said things like, "Stop running!" and "Don't do that!" They seemed like full-blown adults, probably 18 or 19, almost like teachers, but cooler. They were in charge of everything. They taught swimming lessons, made sure we were safe, and let me stay in the pool during the lunch break. I didn't understand why the guards bent the rules for me and showed me this act of kindness. But whatever the reason, I stayed in the water until my skin turned wrinkly and my eyes burned red from the chlorine.

After a long day, I rode my bike home to a big pile of French fries my mom had waiting for me. I ate until all that was left was the greasy paper towel on the bottom of the plate. Falling asleep again with a book on my chest, I woke up the following day, ate a bowl of Froot Loops, rode my bike to the pool, and did it all over again.

Then, while I was in eighth grade in 1972, a big rumor spread that someone had brought a gun to Curtis Junior High. Stories circulated about whether or not a gunshot had been heard. Teachers stood in the hallways and spoke to each other with their hands cupped over their mouths. The music stopped playing during lunch, and I walked past security guards to enter my school.

Everything felt different. I held my books close to my chest and stared at the floor as I walked the hallways. Without *Soul Train,* my favorite part of school was gone.

Soon after the gun rumors, my parents talked about moving. Billboards lined the freeways, selling new homes, fresh air, and safety in Orange County. People like my family living in Los Angeles were sold a vision that life was wonderful and safe south of Disneyland. Our Cairo Avenue home quickly sold, and we traded it for a new one, identical to every fourth house on Via La Coruna in Mission Viejo.

As I left the only home I'd ever known, Billie Jean King beat Bobby Riggs in the historic tennis match, the "Battle of the Sexes." Like the crack of the bat hitting the ball, I watched Billie Jean King swing her tennis racket, taking down Bobby Riggs, and realized there could be a different life waiting for me, a girl.

## *Nadadores*

In Mission Viejo, my red 10-speed Raleigh took me everywhere. One day, instead of turning right on Marguerite Parkway toward town, I turned left. I heard splashing and shouting, so I got off my bike to check it out.

I crawled through a row of bushes and froze. The pool was massive, a hidden place filled with swimmers. They all looked the same—a blur of white arms moving like machines.

To the left was another pool, with diving boards and a tall tower, like the ones I'd seen on TV during the Munich Olympics. I wanted to see a diver climb to the top, stand in front of Saddleback Mountain, and somersault into the water.

This wasn't Victoria Park. But it was a pool—and it was only 10 minutes from my house.

When I got home, I told my dad, "I want to start swimming again."

He offered to take me to the pool. He wasn't a 10-minute-walking kind of man, so we drove to the recreation center. We didn't belong, but my dad marched us past the reception desk and straight to the pool. I froze—it was the most enormous pool I'd ever seen.

Swimmers were crowded into each lane, moving in a

circle, down one side, back on the other. The coach paced the deck in a short-sleeved polo shirt, clipboard in hand and stopwatch swinging from his neck.

Jerry, my dad, an ex-Marine from New York, was bigger in height and girth than the coach. He peppered his talk with Yiddish—"What a meshuga"—his way of reminding you he was part of the tribe. He sold furniture at Levitz, and he'd ask just about everyone he met, "Can I help you buy a couch?"

But today his job was to sell me to this intense, serious-looking man.

"I'm Jerry. And your name is…?" He put out his hand and smiled.

"Coach Mark Schubert," he answered without looking up.

The two men sandwiched me in the middle. "My daughter here is a great swimmer," my dad pointed down at me.

Immediately I felt flushed and shaky, like one of those naked-in-a-grocery-store bad dreams. *I've made a big mistake and want to go home now.* I was wearing a swimsuit, assuming I would just jump in the water and join the other swimmers. It was a Kmart special, green and pink, with flowers and a flimsy plastic belt. To make matters worse, the suit was a heavy-knit material that hung loose on my body. My entire package announced I had no clue.

"Go to the kid pool," Coach Schubert said, gesturing to a third, smaller pool, above and behind us. "Talk to Coach Birch."

I was already afraid of Schubert. My dad shrugged and walked away. He left me standing there, all pink and green, and drove home without me.

Coach Birch, a schoolteacher and part-time swim coach, had dark hair, a mustache, gave me a gentle smile. "Please call me Pat."

At 13, I was already considered old to start swimming on a team. Most competitive swimmers had been training for years.

Coach Birch fast-tracked me to learn all four swim strokes: freestyle, backstroke, breaststroke, and butterfly. He taught me starts off the blocks, flip turns, and helped me put on a latex swim cap to keep my long hair out of my face for the workouts.

Within a month, in the summer of 1973, Pat graduated me and said, "You're ready for the big pool now."

I was relieved to escape the kiddie team. "Mom, I need new swim stuff now that I'm on the senior team. I need a training suit, goggles, and a better swim cap." Asking for money was tough.

"Let me see what I can do, Debbie," which meant she'd have to ask my dad for money.

After dinner, my mom carefully timed her request. She stood to his side, careful not to block the television. With her fingers laced below her waist, she looked submissive and coy at the same time.

"Jerry, I need some money to buy Debbie a training swimsuit and, if it's okay, I'd like to buy some lipstick."

He handed her some money with a terse reminder: "Make

it last."

My face got hot. I was embarrassed and mad—not just for my mom, but for me, too. Before she was married, a new immigrant from Northern Ireland, she had worked as a switchboard operator, pulling and plugging cords into a big board with blinking lights.

Now she was back at it, working at Pacific Bell five days a week, yet she still had to ask my dad for money. I started hiding the money I made from babysitting in my postcard-collection box.

Money in hand, my mom took me shopping to buy me a proper nylon Speedo with a modesty flap—a curious, small piece of material sewn oddly over the pubic mound to hide this unmentionable part of my body.

Ironically, swimming was not a sport for the modest. The boys on the team wore tiny, body-hugging Speedos, shoving their genitals into a tight package to keep everything in place. For women, nylon suits left little to the imagination, exposing every bump, curve, and nipple.

The Nadadores were home to 1972 Olympic medalist Shirley Babashoff, with future Olympians training for the 1976 games. The team was building a reputation as a powerhouse in American swimming, and I showed up unaware, just hoping to make a few new friends.

In the 50-meter pool, the coaches put me in lane eight with the slowest swimmers. No one explained what it meant when I heard a coach shout "10 x 200 meters on three minutes!" I looked at my lane mates for help, but they left the wall every five seconds, before I could squeeze out a question. I swam, out of breath, and chased the toes in front of me.

There was no time to talk during workouts. I heard the coaches yell things like "Ladders" and "IMs." I followed awkwardly and worried I'd be sent back to Pat.

During the brief moments after I pressed myself out of the pool, tearing off my uncomfortable cap as quickly as possible, I met my new teammates. I was surrounded by the young men and women of Lanes 6, 7, and 8—the Junior Team. There were no formal introductions. I was treated as if I'd always been there, as part of the group. It was the first time I'd been accepted and made friends since I'd left Gardena.

When the alarm shook me out of bed at 5:30 in the morning, I got up because I knew my new friends were waiting on the deck of this new water world.

My questions spilled out: "How do I use the pace clock on the deck? What does 'descending' mean?" My teammates piped up all at once to teach me. I gravitated to Kim, another new swimmer, and stayed close.

I learned the silent language we used to communicate during a two-hour workout to avoid getting yelled at by Sheldon, the assistant coach. We knew who liked who and gossiped with quick looks.

Micki swam in front of me, and we both had a few seconds before she left for her next set. In that brief moment, Jesse walked by with a kickboard in hand, and we lit up. There were smiles and extra eye contact between Micki and Jesse, and I was excited and jealous. Then she was off the wall, swimming her 10 x 100 breaststroke set.

In the water, everything and every day on the Nadadores was a competition. Age, gender, and past performance didn't matter. In Lane 8, my job was simple: pass the swimmer in front of me and work my way to the next lane.

Pull sets were about upper-body strength. A black inner tube wrapped around my feet kept my legs still and floated my torso high in the water. We strapped on yellow plastic hand paddles to pull more water and build our shoulder strength. I was a beast, led my lane, and felt proud. I savored these small victories.

Coach Schubert stood at the end of my lane. I could feel him evaluating my potential. He said nothing. I tried to send my message by ESP: "Look at me, look at me."

I finally started to make senior times and gave myself a quick pat on the back, but it was short-lived—on this team, good was never fast enough.


One year after I stepped on the pool deck, swimming consumed my life. I was all in. I trained twice a day, 12 miles a day, six days a week. I carried my yellow time-standard card with the Nadadores team logo on the front and dreamed of making the time standards on the list—Senior, Junior Nationals, Nationals, and the Olympic Trials. The yellow card held the normal expectations for Nadadores swimmers, including me.

After school, I sprinted to workout to avoid the wrath

of the coaches for being late. Before diving into the pool, I started in the weight room every afternoon. Grabbing an empty Nautilus station, I rotated through triceps, biceps, and bench presses—every new idea Schubert had to make us faster and stronger.

With my thighs locked in, I wrapped my hands tight around the lat pulldown bar above my head. For one minute, I pulled and released, grunting and groaning with my teammates. I tried to remember what I'd lifted the day before—and whether I could add 10 more pounds, just to prove I was getting stronger, not falling behind.

My teammates and I meticulously logged every yard swum, every timed set, every pound lifted in our steno notebooks, which we turned in to the coaches each Saturday. Missing a workout wasn't an option, but if we did, we made it up on Sunday.

Following morning workouts, I rushed to stand alone on Marguerite Parkway to catch the 7 a.m. bus to San Clemente High. My hair was wet, and my skin wore the chlorine stench of the pool. I carried two bags—one heavy with swim gear and the other crammed with my lunch, books, and folders. Most of my Nadadores teammates went to Mission Viejo High, just a few minutes away. But because I was new to town and the local schools were full, I was bused to San Clemente, 30 minutes south and a world apart.

San Clemente was a small beach town where everyone

seemed to know each other and looked the same—white skin, blond hair, tanned legs, blue eyes. At my new school, I stood out in a bad way. My best plaid pants, gauzy blouse, and clunky dance shoes screamed "outsider."

The dress code was unwritten but strictly followed. Girls wore halter tops, pastel Ditto pants, and Rainbow sandals. Boys wore surf tees and shorts. The ones in varsity jackets leaned against the quad wall like they owned it. They were the popular guys, and I stayed clear and kept my head down.

As I searched for a way to fit in at my new school, I found no *Soul Train* dancing or swimming pool. My high school had a men's swim team that swam in a pool in town, but no women's team. I was left high and dry, second-class. I was pissed off, stayed quiet, and kept my frustration to myself. My laps with the Nadadores blurred with bus rides, classes, homework, and food. I always wanted more food.

I showed up in my second year at San Clemente High, no longer a lowly freshman, to find a brand-new pool. It came with a pace clock, backstroke flags, and "Warning, No Lifeguard on Duty" signs—all magically built over the summer. Most important, I found a sign-up sheet for a new girl's swim team.

Two years earlier, Congress had passed a law I'd never heard of, but it would change my life. Title IX of the Education Amendments of 1972 was a federal law that required schools and colleges to provide equal opportunities to women and girls in academics and athletics.

Without knowing it, I became one of its first beneficiaries.

Title IX gave me something I hadn't known how to name—something that gnawed at me since I sat on the Little League equipment shed and watched the boys play ball. I knew it wasn't right that the boys had a team and we didn't.

On my new high school team, unlike the Nadadores, the women and men didn't train or compete together; we were kept separate and not quite equal. Mr. Hartman, a seasoned swim coach, led the men. Mrs. Conners was the girls' coach—a P.E. teacher and obviously not a swimmer. Tall and pale, with limp blond hair and a mouth that never smiled, she stood on deck and pointed at the water, "Go back and forth and swim fast."

I gossiped and whispered to my teammates, "Mrs. Conners is the worst; she doesn't know anything—and look at those pants—U G L Y." They laughed and, for a moment, I felt like a popular girl.

When practice started, I waved goodbye to my high school friends and headed for the bus. My real workout, the second one of the day, waited with the Nadadores.

I was allowed to miss Nadadores workouts for high school swim meets. At school, with a brand-new team and pool, I set a school record every time I dove off the starting blocks—because none existed yet. I felt conflicted, knowing there were much faster swimmers who could easily kick my ass. I swam with them every day.

I became known as "that swimmer girl at San Clemente High." It wasn't the same as being popular, but it felt better than being invisible.

I swam competitively through my teen years. My pulse

was in the low 40s—a heartbeat equivalent to a marathon runner's. I could bench-press my 130-pound body weight with ease and crank out sets of push-ups and pull-ups by the dozen.

My shoulders broadened, and my pants got tighter with bigger glutes and hamstrings. Weight training was still relatively new to swimming, and the idea of women bulking up was controversial.

In the locker room, surrounded by other strong girls, I thought my muscled body was normal. But shopping for clothes told a different story. It was a sad affair, a reminder I didn't look like the girls on the cover of *Seventeen* or the ones I sat next to in class. I needed oversized shirts for my swimmer shoulders and pants big enough to contain my strong glutes and butt, yet they all hung loose around my waist. Everything was too big and too small at the same time.

Bras were humiliating. They dug into my shoulders, trying to contain my swimmer's lats, and hung forward awkwardly over my flat chest. I should have skipped the bras. I had no idea women across the country were burning theirs.

At Sears, my mom handed bras over the changing-room stall but wouldn't look inside. It was a guessing game. I stood in the little room without a mirror and heard her say, "Let's try this one."

Like many young women I swam with, I had extremely low body fat. My menstrual cycle didn't start until I was 17. That wasn't unusual for swimmers, but no one talked about it—not parents, not coaches, not doctors. In the 1970s, we lacked the language and science to understand how hormones, body fat, and training schedules influenced our bodies.

I swam forward in silence, unsure of what was normal or what would happen if I started bleeding in the pool.

There was a time of reprieve. Every August, for two weeks, my alarm didn't go off at 5:30 a.m. But I still woke early, confused by the idea of sleeping in. My friends set me straight: it was time for T-Street, a popular beach just south of San Clemente Pier.

We lined up at the bus stop in Mission Viejo and rode to the T-Street stop. Towels in hand, we crossed the pedestrian bridge over the railroad tracks as the Amtrak passed below. On the other side, stairs led to sand and the ocean, waiting just for us. Eileen, Kim, Charlie, and I threw our gear down and sprinted toward the water, wearing saggy bikinis, Speedos, and cut-off shorts.

We knew nothing about rip currents, tides, swells, or blackball flags. No lane lines or coaches were standing above us. I remembered myself as a little girl, running into the ocean and feeling freedom. I wanted to feel that way again.

We shared a few boogie boards and flailed without fins. I dove under waves and popped out the back, trying to get airborne. For a moment, I was a dolphin, sleek, fast, and wild.

The ocean tasted salty. I scrubbed my skin, trying to get rid of the smell of chlorine. As I floated on my back, my legs rose to the surface, buoyed by the ocean water. Back on shore, we tossed our towels in a pile and sat tight, arms and legs tangled like we did at swim meets. I covered myself in baby oil, waited until my skin was pink and sunburned, then ran into the surf again.

In the water, I saw movement beyond the waves. My heart racing, I turned around and screamed at my friends on the beach, "Dolphins, dolphins! Look, real dolphins!"

The T-Street lifeguard left us alone. Or maybe we just didn't notice him. In my wildest thoughts, I couldn't have imagined that one day I'd be working a few towers south, making rescues at San Clemente State Beach.

## *Saddleback*

My shoulders ached with every lap. Each stroke felt like I was pulling tires through the water, and a sense of defeat washed over me. I hadn't reached my goals—not Nationals, not the Olympics. I kept swimming anyway, unsure what else to do.

I graduated from high school in the spring of 1977, and I didn't have plans for a life beyond the pool, so I kept showing up to workouts, my head down in the water, following the black line. I just didn't know what it meant to stop swimming, but I did know that something had changed.

I didn't know what came next, only that I wanted more. I swam my laps without direction or motivation. On a warm Saturday-afternoon workout, Queen stuck in my head, playing over and over—was my life real, or just a fantasy?

At 17, I had never had a beer, a joint, or sex. My girlfriends were teaching me how to use tampons for the first time. My world was small. I wasn't a late bloomer; I was late to life.

Books like *Centennial* and *Siddhartha* offered me glimpses of other lives—distant, confusing, and curious.

After years of workouts, Schubert still paced the deck without making eye contact: "Quit talking and concentrate on the set."

I left the wall to swim my 10 x 100s. Suddenly the water closed in on me, and I felt claustrophobic. I thought about defying the coach, jumping out, and walking away.

Instead, my mind raced, and I imagined arms encircling me from all directions. These were the arms of women I didn't know who had fought for equality before I was born. They lifted me out of the water and onto their shoulders and said, "We fought for you." From the top of their shoulders, I looked at the sky, beyond the black line on the bottom of the pool. I wasn't sure what came next, but I wanted to find out.

I wasn't the only one searching for what came next. The world outside the pool was changing, too.

Before Title IX, sports scholarships for women were almost unheard of. But by the time I graduated from high school, everything had changed. Swim coaches across the country were actively recruiting women like me to build competitive NCAA teams.

Almost every woman I swam with on the Nadadores Senior Team, including me, was offered a swim scholarship to help launch Division I programs. I thought these opportunities were normal. They weren't. We became the living proof, the first women to benefit from Title IX.

Swim Coach Mike Judd at San Diego State University

called with an offer, "Debbie, I can give you admission and a scholarship to swim for San Diego State. This includes books and tuition—about $300 a year." To sweeten the deal, he offered swim gear and paid travel to meets.

A real coach wanted me to swim for a real college. This wasn't pretend anymore. Then Jim and Bev Montrella, from Lakewood Aquatics, told me about their new program at Indian River Community College, in Florida, which would soon become Indian River State College. I liked Bev. She had coached for the Nadadores and was the only woman I'd seen on deck with the team. Petite, friendly, and a swimmer herself. I trusted her.

I hadn't thought much about San Diego. College was still abstract. My parents hadn't gone, and my friends were sorting through their own offers. Florida just sounded more exciting—farther away, more grown up.

It felt simple—I'd follow Bev and Jim. I packed my bags for Florida, all based on Bev's smile. But reality sank in as the date got closer. I had no money, no plan, and no idea of how to pay for anything beyond what the scholarship covered. At the last minute, I chickened out and declined the offer. I wasn't ready. I didn't know how to be on my own yet.

With nowhere else to go, and no desire to return to the Nadadores, I enrolled at Saddleback Community College. I skipped scholarships and Division I swimming, stayed in town to grow up, get a date, and make some money. Saddleback checked all those boxes.

That fall of 1977, I walked onto a new pool deck.

Saddleback Mountain still loomed, but from a new angle. The scent of tobacco hit me before I saw Coach Flip Darr and his iconic pipe.

"I'm Debbie Friedman, a Mission Viejo Nadador. I'd like to join the swim team."

Saddleback College was full of young and energetic teachers just starting their careers. Bill and Robin Valencic, a husband-and-wife team, taught Coastal Ecology of Southern California. They took us to Dana Point, and we walked gently over slippery rocks and through tide pools, identifying hermit crabs, sea anemones, sea stars, and limpets.

Human Anatomy became my favorite class. One day we went to the lab—a cold room that smelled like formaldehyde. Our teacher, Mr. Childers, a smiling, short, stocky, bald man, said, "If you feel faint, just leave the room."

A man in a white gown rolled out a shiny metal drawer and unzipped the plastic bag. The cadaver was placed under bright lights as the assistant opened flaps of precut skin and pointed out the ribcage, kidneys, liver, and heart. A small cloth covered his genitals. Mr. Childers calmly explained each organ as it was revealed.

The poor dead guy had done this act many times before. When it was over, they folded him neatly back into the bag, zipped it up, and slid him into the wall again, ready for the next group. *Would Mr. Childers donate his body to a class someday?* He did look a bit like the corpse.

I had seen a human body from the inside out, and I wanted to see more.

I became a wide-eyed little kid again, looking at the world

through a gyroscope, learning something new every day. My awakening followed me to the water.

Early in the season, Flip asked each team member, "What are your goals?"

When it was my turn to sit down with him, I was at a loss for words.

He answered for me. "There are no time standards here, Debbie. We'll talk later about the level of competition you'll face at the State Championship. Right now, enjoy yourself. The team's going to love you."

My shoulders dropped, and I teared up. For the first time in years, a coach had looked at me instead of a clipboard full of times. I'd made the right move.

I fell in love with the water again, not just as a swimmer, but as a person. I could finally breathe. At Saddleback the men and women trained and traveled together, like the Nadadores—but now the theme was fun. Every swimmer mattered. Flip's workouts were tough, but with less yardage and more recovery time. He was big on personal choice. If you had goals, he showed you how to reach them. And if you didn't follow through?

"Then I guess that's not your goal," he'd say, as he sat on the deck, smoking his pipe.

We cracked jokes between sets, grabbing and teasing each other without getting scolded. And sex? I was no longer a simple robot swimming laps. I felt my face flush as I pressed in tight against the others on the wall. The air was charged with physicality. This wasn't the sterile, rule-bound world of the Nadadores. I swam hard, laughed loud, and let myself look at the men's bodies beside me. Having fun wasn't against the rules.

We piled into school vans and crisscrossed the state, competing against other community colleges. On deck, we stood shoulder to shoulder and cheered every teammate, from the slowest to the fastest.

Erin pressed in close beside me, Kenny blasted Led Zeppelin, and Brian grinned like he was up to something. They weren't just teammates. They were friends.

Before the State Championships, we carbo-loaded, shoving plates of spaghetti and French fries into our bodies, convinced they were elixirs of fuel for speed. Beer, as always, was justified as an important carb.

And then, the shave-down. At Kenny's mom's house, we gathered with Bic razors to strip every hair from our bodies—at least the parts not covered by our skinsuits. As we helped each other reach the spots we couldn't get to alone, the Eagles' *Hotel California* blasted through the room. The smell of pot mixed with the stink of thick, foamy shaving cream. What began as a serious pre-race ritual turned into a full-blown shaving-cream war—faces, bodies, and Kenny's mom's brown shag carpet didn't stand a chance.

The next day, I stood on the starting block, waiting to hear: "Swimmers, take your marks." My suit compressed my body so tightly that it appeared I had no breasts. I stood tall, locked on the far end of the pool, and dismissed my competition. I became a hydrodynamic, lean, mean swimming machine.

I didn't know how strong I was until after I left the

Nadadores. For the first time since Victoria Park, I rediscovered my passion for swimming. With Flip's coaching and the camaraderie of my new teammates, I thrived—and won a few state titles for community-college swimming. I was a big fish in a little pond. But I was fast, and I was finally having fun.

I bonded closely with my new teammates. At first, I was cautious, feeling like a child meeting grown-ups. The men, for the most part, were fully grown and had lives and interests beyond swimming. The women joined the team for all kinds of reasons—fitness, camaraderie, or simply for fun. The biggest surprise was the lack of conformity among the people I was meeting. My teammates didn't just accept differences—they celebrated them. For the first time, people were curious about my life beyond the pool.

I could talk about things I'd read, but I didn't have many original ideas to share. My world had been swimming. I woke up, trained, ate, and went to sleep. But I wanted more. I just didn't know what.

Right off the bat, I met Erin Porter and we became fast friends. Her smile and laughter were infectious. She lived a few miles down the road, in San Juan Capistrano. Her hair was sun-bleached blond, different from my chlorine-streaked, straw-textured blond, even green-tinted in some lighting. Erin was a couple of inches shorter and 40 pounds lighter. Where I was all muscle from years in the weight room, she was lithe and graceful.

Before Erin spoke, she giggled and lowered her eyes. *Maybe she's shy.* I tried to figure her out. I quickly learned it was a false front. Pound for pound, Erin was a beast of a competitor. During workouts, Erin was first in the water and last out, always with a smile. She pulled into the parking lot in her yellow Mustang with a surfboard strapped to the roof.

The only surfer I could name was Jerry Lopez, Mr. Pipeline. I watched him on *Wide World of Sports* as he defied death and the sharp coral reef below his board, surfing the hollow waves on the North Shore of Hawai'i.

I watched Erin; *I've never known a woman who surfs.*

Every teammate brought something unique. Kenny was a strong backstroker who arrived with wild curly hair and a matching smile. Brian, all unkempt dark hair and lanky limbs, drove a tan El Camino and spent his free time smoking pot and tossing Frisbees. I was attracted to his car, and then to him, the bad boy.

While drying off after a swim workout, I heard one of the guys announce, "My place, party tonight. Let me know if you need directions." *Did this mean I'm invited?*

I had been teaching swimming at the rec center and had saved enough money for my first car, a green Dodge Colt—my independence. I fired up the Green Booger and drove to the party house.

Inside, David Bowie sang from the turntable, beer flowed, weed wafted, and the dancing turned into a full-on free-for-all. Bodies crashed into each other, arms and legs moving at high speed. I kicked off my sandals and danced barefoot on the sticky linoleum. With abandon, like my Motown days at Curtis Junior High, I shut my eyes and moved to the music, lost in the moment. Van Morrison slowed us down with *Moondance*, and the energy shifted. I moved slower and pulled in closer with the tangle of bodies. There was life beyond swimming.

Scott Stuart, one of the older swimmers—mid-20s, maybe—hung back at workouts, lingering on the fringes of our group. At parties, he arrived late and left early. He wasn't shy, just distant, aloof—as if his thoughts were elsewhere.

One-on-one, he paid attention to me and had opinions on swimming, politics, and what I should read.

"*Zen and the Art of Motorcycle Maintenance* would be good for you," he'd say, raising an eyebrow. When I asked him questions, he'd laugh: "Does it even matter? None of this is real anyway."

He had sandy-colored chest hair, rare among swimmers. One day he'd want to talk and hang out; the next, he'd pass me like I didn't exist. I followed him around like a lost puppy dog. I took mental notes on everything he said, like a disciple with her guru.

It was February 1978, and swim season was in full swing. Scott looked at me with a mischievous grin: "Come take the lifeguard swim test at Huntington State Beach tomorrow." I hung onto every word. "I've been a lifeguard at San Clemente for three summers," he added. "It's a good job—pays $5.10 an hour."

Scott didn't mention that there were no women lifeguards at San Clemente State Beach, and I didn't think to ask. I had never imagined a world without women swimmers.

Scott said I should go, so I went.

The following morning, I drove alone to Huntington

State Beach. When I arrived, I didn't see Scott anywhere. There was no check-in or forms to fill out. I followed the crowd in my one-piece suit, hair tied back in a rubber band. Soon I stood barefoot in the cold sand, on the starting line, surrounded by a hundred men in Speedos.

*Where were the other women? Why am I the only one here? Did I make a mistake?*

I put my head down, looked at my body, and was aware that I was different. I wasn't clear on the racecourse, but my brain shifted into race mode. I looked up and down at my competitors; a few of the men wore trunks, and I saw them as easy targets to swim past, their baggy suits slowing them down.

*Deep breaths, in and out.* I knew how to swim fast.

A megaphone shouted loud, squeaky instructions: "Swim out to the red buoy, 500 yards out. Turn around it on your left shoulder, and then back to shore. Remember, only the top swimmers will qualify."

I could barely see the buoy as the gun went off, signaling us to run and swim like hell.

The water was cold, but after a few strokes, my nerves melted. I targeted and passed every man in front of me, and found myself turning the buoy with the lead pack. This world I knew. It was time to race for the finish.

4

# *Does Size Matter?*

*Wendy*

Wendy Paskin bent into the water, grabbed a fellow rookie, slung one of his arms over her shoulder, shoved her hips into his waist, and heaved him sideways over her back. Then she trudged him to shore. It was like carrying someone piggyback, but sideways, through foamy whitewater, sand, and laughter, mostly at her expense.

Wendy wore her nylon stars-and-stripes Speedo, a suit made for nationally ranked swimmers. To prove she had the manly-man strength needed to become the first woman lifeguard for Los Angeles County in 1974, she was required to lug a big male up the beach. The lugging was called the Saddleback Carry.

The carry wasn't some long-standing lifeguard tradition

51

handed down from the rope-and-reel days. The test was created just for women. It came from old military rescue drills, where a casualty was thrown over the rescuer's back and hauled to safety. Somehow that became a rite of passage for women lifeguards.

For me, Saddleback seemed to follow wherever I went—first the mountain I swam beneath as a Nadador, then the college that brought me back to loving the water, and now, a nonsensical lifeguard test of strength.

Lifeguard Chief Bob Burnside and Department of Beaches Director Dick Fitzgerald added the carry specifically for Wendy—a test that Los Angeles County Lifeguards had never required before. Burnside said he supported hiring women, but behind closed doors, he was afraid that women weren't strong enough and told Fitzgerald, "I'm worried about our standards."

I pictured a chalkboard as they brainstormed ideas: *Push a jeep through the sand. Clean a toilet while carrying a guard on her shoulders. Open a beer with one hand.* Instead, they went with the Saddleback Carry. After considering a version with one arm tied behind her back, they settled on the military model.

Other lifeguard agencies thought it was a good idea and followed like lemmings, adding the carry to their training programs. The guards in charge enjoyed the sight of rookies—especially the women rookies—hauling each other out of the surf while they laughed from the sand.

During my rookie training in 1978, I faced the same test. Tom was a San Diego State guy who must have weighed three hundred pounds, give or take a hundred. He was a giant. I looked high into the sky at his red hair and freckled face and tried to exude confidence that I could carry him safely to shore. Almost every woman guard I talked to told me, "My partner was the biggest guy in my rookie class."

All eyes were on me, the only woman. Half the class wanted to see me succeed, the other half wanted me to drop him, hoping for a car-crash moment with blood and guts.

I carried Tom to shore through the surf zone and set him down gently in front of our classmates. He blushed. The carry wasn't a macho-man thing; it was more like a party trick—flipping an unsuspecting guy with a red plastic cup up and over my back, spilling his beer.

But on the dry sand, as I stood there soaking wet, my thin nylon suit clinging to my skin—breasts, belly button, and pubic hair visible through the fabric, I felt naked, singled out as different.

I'd never seen it used in a real ocean rescue. If the men in charge wanted a tougher test for us, they should've added walking on water.


The test—the Saddleback Carry—had been required for Wendy Paskin, Los Angeles County's first woman lifeguard, in 1974. But all the fretting over how women could prove their strength had already been played out a year earlier, when Kiane Nowell faced the same challenge for the Los Angeles City Lifeguards.

## *Kiane*

In 1973, Kiane Nowell, at 5-foot-2 and 103 pounds, hoisted her 175-pound classmate over her back and trudged him through the surf to shore, right in front of Venice Lifeguard Headquarters.

The training lieutenant from Playa Del Rey, standing with his hand on his chin, said, "Well done, that's far enough. You can put him down now."

At the time, Kiane, 21, was competing for the Santa Monica City College swim team. Her boyfriend was a lifeguard, and she swam laps with guards. These new friends watched her pound out the laps and swim the same workouts alongside them. Drying off on the deck after a workout, a chorus of male voices chanted, "Kiane, come take the lifeguard test."

Unlike some agencies, Los Angeles City lifeguards didn't list "men only" requirements. They focused solely on a competitive run-swim-run, with no height or weight restrictions.

Kiane arrived at Cabrillo Beach in San Pedro. The 1,000-yard buoy marker was in place. She took her place on the starting line and saw only men to her right and left. She felt vibes that said, "Move out of the way."

Out of 200 men who swam the race, she beat more than 160 of them, earning a coveted spot in lifeguard training.

Reporters and TV cameras came to film as she finished the swim. With cameras aimed at her, reporters yelled, "Kiane, Kiane, how does it feel to be the first woman lifeguard?"

She passed lifeguard training with high marks and became the first woman lifeguard for the City of Los Angeles.

In 1973, as you sat and ate your Cheerios in the morning, you might have seen Kiane tell her story on *The Today Show*, with more than one million television viewers.

*Parade* magazine, one of the country's most widely read Sunday weeklies, put Kiane on its cover, standing strong, proud, holding a rescue buoy next to a lifeguard truck.

A Los Angeles newspaper headlined, "Libbers Score Again." With a brief introduction and a picture of Kiane kneeling in her swimsuit, the article mocked her, "Kiane is assigned to the city beach at Venice for those who would like to be rescued."

She finished in the top 10 in her rookie class. Traditionally, this high score gave a guard preference for choosing which beach to work.

Kiane picked Will Rogers Beach, near her home in Pacific Palisades. Families in wood-paneled station wagons came to Will Rogers to enjoy the stunning views and picnic on the quiet beach. Catalina Island sat offshore on a clear day, and the Palos Verdes Peninsula unfolded to the south. Behind Pacific Coast Highway, the Santa Monica Mountains rose steeply.

The lieutenant in charge of Will Rogers Beach was a World War II veteran responsible for his stretch of coast and anyone who set foot on it. When Kiane showed up as a new rookie lifeguard, he looked at her, then let his gaze travel slowly down her body to her feet before bringing it back, just as slowly, to the top of her head. With his hands on his khaki hips, he said, "I don't want you here."

Kiane clenched her jaw; she was pissed.

She was left waiting for a willing male supervisor to give her the nod to climb into a tower and work.

"Not on my beach," she was told by guys who peed on their fire hydrants, protecting the past.

Kiane was eventually allowed to work at Venice Beach. "OK," the Lifeguard Captain said. "We'll see if it works out."

Venice was a crowded, gritty beach with much more rescue action than Will Rogers. To reach her tower, Kiane walked through Muscle Beach, the training ground for the world's top bodybuilders, including seven-time Mr. Olympia Arnold Schwarzenegger.

She climbed into her tower and watched her water while a parade of counter-culture chaos cruised the beach. Behind her tower, on the boardwalk, Black Panthers walked past surfer dudes, and monks paused to watch jugglers. The Doors were legendary in Venice, and everywhere you turned, guitar players sang, "Come on, baby, light my fire…" In her tower, she could hear mufflers rev from the streets as motorcycle clubs became part of the scene.

"That first summer," Kiane laughed as we shared coffee decades later, "Venice was getting a reputation as a place to go nude."

"Guys would come to my tower naked and ask me to put on their sunscreen."

Kiane lives near me in the Monterey Bay area, and I was thrilled to meet her in person.

"What was working as a first woman lifeguard like, given your size?" I wasn't sure what word to use. *Should I call her short, petite, or small?* I stayed with the generic "size."

At 72, Kiane peppered her stories with "that SOB" and "that guy was cool." She never once expressed any doubt about her ability to do the job. Size was not her issue; it was theirs.

As we talked, she stood up and pushed her coffee aside. Arms swinging, she started, "One of my toughest rescues was an entire family pulled offshore by a rip current. I swam far beyond the surf line to rescue all four of them. I had each hang on to part of my buoy, calmed them down, and pulled the entire family to shore. I'll never forget it."

There were problems. She remembered one of the "SOBs" in great detail.

"Chief O'Henry threatened me over dress codes, long hair, and swimsuit styles. He wrote me up once for taking a shower alone in the locker room at 5 p.m., apparently without the official pretty-please request. I refused to sign the reprimand." As she relived the injustice, her voice sharpened.

I told Kiane that when I became a permanent lifeguard at Huntington Beach, I received a "needs improvement" mark on the quality and cleanliness of my dress uniform. It felt like a reprimand. I had the same dress uniform as the men lifeguards—worn to funerals and special events. Not that I'd attended any yet. The special outfit was a white-collared dress shirt with a blue-and-gold bear patch on one sleeve and a pair of dark-blue pressed Dickies-style pants. My boss and evaluator, Roger, said I needed to wear a skirt.

"What skirt? Where do I buy this skirt, Roger?"

I was the only woman permanent lifeguard in State Parks, and nobody had told me about the skirt. I looked at him across the table, and his expression was dead serious. He wasn't joking. With no solution or offer to improve my score, I was marked down because Roger wanted to wear the pants in the family.

The evaluation was meaningless, and there was no skirt, but every time I looked at Roger afterward, something was off. He played by his own small, strange rulebook.

Kiane switched the conversation to the cool stuff: memories of the actual work of lifeguarding. She told me about some "crazy" rescues she had made.

"Before work, I was doing a swim-and-run workout near my tower. An engine sputtered, and I looked out at the water. A single-engine plane appeared and fell nose first out of the sky and into the ocean."

A plane going down in front of a tower or a boat landing on a beach was out of scale, like watching a movie in a theater with Hitchcock's birds coming off the screen and into your face. But within a nanosecond, a shake of the head, a lifeguard responds.

"My mind reacted," Kiane recalled. "I grabbed my buoy and ran through the surf toward the plane."

Thankfully, so did other lifeguards, firefighters, the Coast Guard, Harbor Patrol, paramedics, ambulance trucks, and anyone else called to duty.

Kiane's small size was difficult to reconcile without feeding into every stereotype I feared. As I learned about Kiane, though, I re-examined my ideas about size.

When I started lifeguarding, I was 5-foot-7, thick, strong, and a mass of muscles. I was bigger than many of the men I worked with—but I wasn't the biggest woman lifeguard. Women came to lifeguarding in all shapes and sizes. Sally Tuttle, from Ventura State Beach, stood 6-foot-1.

Among the first women guards, all of us were larger than Kiane. But later, in the 1980s, when I trained seasonal lifeguards, I saw rookies of every shape and size, men and women alike. Quietly, I kept questions about a few smaller women to myself. But I carried an extra layer of judgment toward women guards already facing extra hoops to jump through.

The truth was, I'd thought about these women the same way the men did. *Is she strong or small? Short or thin? I'll need to keep an extra close eye on this one.* I had questions about men, too, but they usually related to the size of their brains.

Kiane changed how I thought about strength and size.

She was a top finisher in her training class. Instructors scored rookies on rescues, tests, swims, runs, first aid, and even how quickly they cleaned the training rooms and toilets. Any sign of disrespect or poor attitude was reason enough to fail.

Instructors wrote numbers in columns, commented in margins, and tallied scores, but in the end, they could still write in the tidy score book, "Based on my years of experience, this candidate does not have the right stuff to be a lifeguard."

It wasn't about the numbers. It was who the instructors believed could be a lifeguard.

Once rookies like Kiane—who finished 10th in her class—passed training, it was up to the beach mentors and supervisors to help new guards build skills and confidence. The question should not have been, "Could she be a lifeguard?" It should have been, "How can we support this lifeguard to become the best guard possible?"

Kiane made me examine my thinking and broaden my understanding of what it takes to become an accomplished lifeguard. She showed up early as a woman lifeguard to deliver the in-your-face truth that size does not matter.

## *Panther Girl*

People have always measured things to make sense of the world. It allowed us to find certainty when there was none. Lifeguards measured things all the time. We assessed the size of the surf and the wind's velocity, tallied the number of daily rescues, and logged water temperatures. Many beaches even ranked lifeguards with numbers to give better schedules to the top dogs in the pecking order.

We also used measurements to help us describe and communicate our instructions, thoughts, and ideas to one another. Assigned as lifeguard dispatcher for the day, I coordinated all the responses between the lifeguards, the public, and emergency services high on the bluff overlooking San Clemente State Beach. My radio call to the unit below was a mix of numbers, distance, and language shortcuts—"4505, respond to Tower 5, guard out, three victims, 200 yards straight out, Tower 4 responding as backup."

Lifeguard rookies received times for buoy swims and run-swim-runs, plus scores from written tests and first-aid scenarios. These numbers were logged in record books to determine who passed training and got hired.

However, these measurements did not capture the *essence* of a successful lifeguard. The true measure of a lifeguard wasn't quantifiable through simple metrics. Intangible qualities—integrity, empathy, kindness, courage, and respect—defined a lifeguard's success. Logbooks didn't have lines to record these measurements.

Calla Allison was named after her great-grandmother and, fittingly, shares a name with Queen Calafia, the mythical namesake of California. When I thought about what makes a great lifeguard, Calla immediately came to mind.

A few years ago, we talked about a rescue she'd made on a stretch of unguarded coastline—a call-out that stuck with her. And with me.

Calla was a highly skilled state park lifeguard for 16 seasons along the entire coast of Santa Cruz County. "Panther Girl" was her nickname, earned after her daring rescues on the North Coast, including Panther Beach.

Unlike guarded beaches where a family could set up camp under a lifeguard tower and watch patrol vehicles drive back and forth, preventing accidents, the North Coast was only a "call-out" response. This meant that if something went wrong, lifeguards were called to the scene after it happened.

One of the many rescues Calla shared with me took place after a long shift at Seabright State Beach. Just as she was about to go off duty, the dispatcher's voice came over the radio. "Respond Code 3 to Panther Beach." Calla jumped back in her lifeguard truck, turned on her lights and sirens, and drove north.

Panther Beach was about eight miles beyond Santa Cruz, on the remote, rugged, rocky, and dangerous North Coast. The sun dropped low in the sky at dusk, the light fading fast. When Calla arrived on the scene as the sole responding lifeguard, she saw firefighters pointing at two people trapped in a sea cave below the bluffs at Panther Beach.

Waves pounded the couple into a sea cave, slamming them against the sharp rocks at the base of the bluff. The tide was rising—they were trapped in a space that was rapidly filling with water, and if help didn't come immediately, they would drown. The firefighters, unable to rig a safe descent down the cliff face, watched helplessly from above. After a quick assessment, Calla knew she had to get in the water. Fast.

A tattered rope attached to a rock hung over the cliff face. She realized that must have been how the victims had climbed to the beach, now gone with the incoming tide. Calla had her wetsuit on and was "rescue ready," as guards say—ready to go, not mucking around with gear.

She wrapped her fins and rescue tube around her waist and made a leap of faith, grabbing the rope and lowering herself down the 30-foot sandstone wall—the height of a two-story building.

Calla did not wait for a safety line, a harness, or a belay system to descend the bluff to the sharp reef below. Without a safety system, she held the untested rope and turned to face the jagged, crumbling sandstone cliff wall. In position, she gripped the rope, moving each hand below the other and using her feet to stabilize herself against the cliff. She lowered herself, hand by hand, grip by grip, hoping the rope would not give way.

The firefighters, in full turnout gear, watched from above.

She survived the descent with the rope intact and stood on the shallow rocky bottom, with surf ready to hurl her against the cliff face. She let the water come to her and used the swell to carry her out of the dangerous shallows. Rolling on her back, she quickly put the fins on her feet. She heard the screams and could see the entrance to the cave and knew her victims were inside.

"I'm almost there," she yelled into the cave, swimming straight to the entrance.

The cave was dark and disorienting. Crashing waves and screams echoed off the walls, coming at her from all directions.

Calla braced her rescue tube against her chest to protect herself from the cave's jagged walls. She reached the two crying victims and yelled, "I'm going to get you out of here. Hold onto this tube, and no matter what, don't let go!"

She pulled, pushed, and towed her victims through the pounding surf and into what little light was left in the sky.

In the cold open water, holding the two victims, Calla briefly considered the situation: *This is not good.*

Before she could figure out the next steps, she saw the yellow bow of Surfwatch, the lifeguard rescue boat, racing toward them.

Calla and the boat operator loaded the victims on the boat and wrapped them in blankets. The sky was now dark, and these two people needed immediate medical attention. The rescue boat sped a mile north to Red, White, and Blue Beach, where they were met by firefighters, paramedics, and an ambulance.

When the rescue was "Code 4," meaning everyone was safe, Calla was returned to Panther Beach to retrieve her lifeguard truck. She was cold, tired, and ready to go off duty.

A group of firefighters remained at Panther Beach, and one of the men approached her. "Would you like to grab a coffee sometime?" Calla rolled her eyes, laughed, and left him hanging.

Was this really what the firefighter was thinking as he watched the scene unfold below? An offer to clean her lifeguard truck and equipment would have been much more helpful.

Calla saved the drowning couple and, thankfully, her own life that day. No matter how well trained, a lifeguard has no guarantee of safety. For these two people facing death, Calla appeared out of nowhere during the most frightening moments in their lives, moments that might have been their last. They didn't know that Calla had been a college NCAA Division I water-polo player, an Olympic contender, a world bodysurfing champion, and a lifeguard training instructor.

Calla cared deeply about the people she saved and risked her own life to save them. As the cave walls closed in and the water rose, the only thing that mattered was the size of Calla's heart.

5

*Rookie*

## *Training*

All I had to do was survive the sixth and final day of lifeguard training. My towel and swimsuit were still wet from the first day of class. Sand lived in my hair, ears, crotch, and bed. I was exhausted. I saw big plates of steaming French fries and juicy hamburgers on the horizon where the ocean met the sky. I ran miles in the soft sand daily with the other trainees, part of our rescue training.

My calves seized, every step twitching with the threat of a full-blown cramp. I limped until the instructor told me to run again. I thought I knew pain from swimming miles, but this new level of pain humbled me. In the training room, my head dipped forward again and again, and I struggled to hold it up long enough to watch the seconds crawl by.

At some point today, I reassured myself, lifeguard training will end.

For one week in the spring of 1978, 28 lifeguard wannabes, including me, reported to the training room at 8 a.m. sharp. If we weren't on time, we'd fail training and leave in a walk of shame—head down, disgraced, past the smirks and judgment of everyone: *You are not lifeguard material.* I wasn't going to be that person, and I set my alarm for 6:30 a.m., twice.

Each day, more seats were empty. No one told us why.

The training room was the lifeguard garage for vehicles and equipment. In the early morning, real lifeguards drove the jeeps out, while we, the rookies, set up the transformation. We placed small desks and chairs, meant for school kids, in neat rows. They were uncomfortable and ridiculous as I squeezed my body into the small space.

Next to the garage was the small and simple concrete lifeguard administrative office, a white-stucco building with emerald-green trim, located at the intersection of Beach Boulevard and Pacific Coast Highway, the entrance to Huntington State Beach.

Two weeks prior, after the swim and run parts of the tryouts, I'd lined up to enter this little white building for the interview part of the exam. I was wet, shaking, and bundled in my Saddleback swim-team sweatsuit, waiting for my turn to tell the supervising lifeguards what I thought I knew.

Half the hundred men who tried out did not score high enough on the swims and runs to qualify for the interview.

I had been the only woman—and remained the only woman—still standing.

"Debora Friedman? Follow me."

I entered the building and sat before three men. I cleared my throat and wished I saw a woman at the table.

The men deciding my fate were seated behind a desk with pads of paper and coffee mugs. They wore white-collared, pressed uniform shirts and silver-plated name tags on their front pockets. A patch with a golden bear on all fours had the words: California State Park Lifeguard.

They introduced themselves, but I immediately forgot their names. One of the men had a dark, straggly beard and greasy-looking hair. None of the swimmers I knew had beards. Swimmers wanted to be hydrodynamic. I avoided making eye contact with the greasy man. He didn't look like he could swim very fast. To steady myself and quiet my inner ramblings, I placed my hands on my quads. I could see their mouths move, but I didn't hear any words.

*Debbie, pay attention, pull yourself together.*

Refocused, my voice shook as I answered a question about my experience as a swim teacher. I wasn't sure it was going well when I heard myself say, "I don't know how to surf."

Another question came to me: "What will you do if you see an illegal alien?" I'd just seen *Close Encounters of the Third Kind.*

Too quickly, I answered, "What's an illegal alien?"

I told them I needed a summer job, was a strong swimmer, and wanted to help people. The next day, I got a call. "You passed tryouts. Report to training on March 20, 8 a.m., Huntington State Beach."

I hung up the phone, relieved and surprised that I passed. *I can't wait to tell Scott at swim workout tomorrow.*

Every day in training, we started with a "vitamin," a mile run on the beach to the Magnolia HQ lifeguard tower. We entered the water, raced a 1,000-yard swim, tryouts all over again, and ran back to the garage. Every run, swim, drill, written exam, and mock rescue was graded and critiqued. We didn't smile or laugh—this was all business, and the expectations were to carry ourselves as adults, even though at the age of eighteen, I had not entirely passed that threshold.

Every morning, my pulse raced and my hands shook as I fumbled with the rubber band to keep my hair in a tight ponytail.

I was surprised to be the only woman in the class. I didn't understand why lifeguards were exclusively male. I knew little about the job, but I saw no women teaching, driving the jeeps, or working in the lifeguard towers. I sat in a classroom of all men, my competition.

In between lectures, I looked around the room at the crowd of men surrounding me. I had no experience processing what it meant to be the only woman in a class of 28. I searched my mind, trying to figure out how I was supposed to feel. *Was anyone staring at me? How should I act? Do I pretend it's no big deal? Where are the other women?*

My competitive nature put these feelings aside most of the day, and once I was in the water, I wanted to pass the swimmer in front of me. I beat most of the men in my training class during the swims. Years of swimming miles with the Mission Viejo Nadadores gave me a strength advantage. Even in the cold, choppy March water, when the ocean couldn't decide if it was winter or spring, my stroke and body position felt more natural in the salty, buoyant ocean than in the pool.

Something clicked, and I realized all those pool laps had made me strong in the ocean. I was built for this.

We swam without wetsuits or fins, and, with a bit more body fat than most of the men, my body rode high in the water. My head naturally followed my arms up and around to grab a breath, giving me a solid spatial sense of where I was in the water. I was aggressive. The previous summer, I'd swum a couple of pier races and found out it was kosher to grab the swimmer in front of me, pulling them back while I propelled myself forward. I swam my daily "vitamin" by grabbing, pulling, and pushing my competition behind me to secure as much of a lead as I could in the swims before I started running.

I'd never been a runner, and I paid the price. My bare feet were pink, even delicate, and had no calluses to protect me from surfaces harder than water. During the morning vitamins, I managed to gut out the run and stayed with the back of the pack. After entering the water, I caught up and swam with the leaders. Running was always the hardest part.

My skin was raw and chafed where my nylon swimsuit ground against my thighs, glutes, and hips. I tried to see if the men in my class had the same problems, but I couldn't look too long to compare rub marks without my intentions becoming suspect. I didn't have a confidante to help me with red, inflamed welts on my inner thighs. It appeared the other men were not talking to each other about their sore and tender body parts. Women shared this kind of information. Maybe men didn't. I wanted to throw away my swimsuit, burn it, and take a bath in Neosporin.

But I was resilient. "Sit up straight, stay awake, SWIM FAST," was my training mantra.

As part of our cardiopulmonary resuscitation (CPR) training, we were paired up on the beach and instructed, "One of you will swim out past the surf zone and become the victim. Your partner will swim out with his rescue buoy and bring you, the victim, to shore while performing mouth-to-mouth resuscitation."

CPR wasn't a laughing matter. We worked on mannequins to practice the lifesaving technique that pumps a person's heart and gives oxygen to their brain when they might otherwise be dead.

"Check your hand position on the sternum, 15 compressions, and then two breaths," an instructor said. He walked through our practice area, grading us on our technique.

My arms were tired from repeating the straight-armed compressions, pumping one hand on top of the other, squeezing the heart between the sternum and the spine. After a round of 15 compressions, the second rescuer breathed deeply twice, directly into "Annie," the mannequin's mouth, and we repeated the cycle until we were told to stop. I rotated to my new position and breathed twice into Annie as we practiced and took turns swapping each other's saliva.

Back on the beach, it was time to practice mouth-to-mouth resuscitation on a victim in the water. The rookies mobbed me, all wanting to be my partner. No one wanted to lip-lock with another guy. The instructors laughed; they thought it was funny. And I laughed because I was embarrassed. Underneath the show, I was furious, with no one to tell.

I went out with the first round of victims and my designated partner, Tom, who swam out to rescue me. He wrapped me in his rescue tube, floating me face up. We both believed the instructors could see us all the way from shore, and in that nanosecond, Tom opened his mouth as wide as he could. I tried to make mine small enough for him to get a seal. Warm air filled my mouth as he blew into me, over and over. It was awful; a mix of warm spit and saltwater shoved into my mouth. We were both scared as he pulled me in, trying to keep up the make-believe rescue breathing. I saw the shore, my salvation, while coughing up the forced air and salt water.

Suddenly, an inside wave slammed us both into the sandy bottom. Tom's teeth crashed into my mouth, and I reached shore with a bloody lip. Everyone was watching us. There were a few laughs about my lip as blood mixed with the water and ran down my chin. No one offered me a tissue or anything else to stop the bleeding.

*What did they think—this was a date?*

The drill was finally over, and it became clear to me that everything I did was being watched and judged because I'd become the class *female.*

*Just leave me alone so I can kick your ass in the water.*

Every day, I ran to the garage as ordered. It reeked of stale air, body odor, and damp clothes. All of us had been sharing one toilet outside, and the foul smell somehow joined the offensive olfactory cocktail inside and made it worse.

It was also a time of relief. I could dry off, warm up, and rest my legs. With shaky hands, I took notes and listened to lectures on first aid, lifeguard procedures, rules, and regulations.

I looked for moments to make contact with my classmates, time for a brief chat, or some acknowledgment of the shared pain we endured. But no one looked up; the other rookies stared straight ahead with blank, glazed faces.

I did make friends. State Parks gave us money and a travel allowance to stay in a local Newport Dunes motel. Before the first day of training, Kim Raymont, my good friend from Nadadores, told me about two of her San Diego State swim friends who would be in the same class.

"I checked with George and Brian," she told me, "and they are okay if you stay with them."

If I shared their room, I could pocket the leftover travel money.

"Sounds good to me," I replied.

After another nonstop day, my body dragging, the short instructor with the high-pitched voice gave us his usual send-off: "Clean up your gear, put the chairs away, and be here at 8 a.m. tomorrow."

George, Brian, and I piled into my Dodge Colt and headed to the motel. We bought burritos and ate them before we made it to our room.

"Who's your favorite teacher?" I asked.

"They are all losers, but Carl isn't a jerk," George grinned.

We joked about the fastest swimmer, how to survive the runs, and then I heard snoring. Brian was on the floor, a wet towel under his head and a polyester bedspread over his body. He was fast asleep.

The days blurred until it was the final day of training. The clock dragged as 6 p.m. approached. The instructors stood before us and made final remarks: "… lives are at stake."

At last we were dismissed. No handshakes, no congratulations. The only way I knew I passed was that I hadn't failed. It was anticlimactic. One of the biggest things I'd ever accomplished in my life, and I was left alone to pack up my gear.

I needed Big Macs and sleep. I needed to read my water-stained notes and make sense of all the information thrown at me. Over and over again, I was told that if I didn't remember this or that, someone was going to die on my watch. Those words went straight to my heart.

I bargained with myself: If I could eat and sleep, I would memorize all my notes, do all the right things. Outside the training room, I staggered to my car.

Carl Drake, one of the instructors, walked up to me, "I need you to report for duty at San Clemente State Beach tomorrow. Starting time is 9 a.m. Go to Tower 1."

I started to shake. But not from fatigue or hunger. I was working as a lifeguard tomorrow. I looked at my teacher and nodded, "Carl, where is Tower 1?"

## *Easter Sunday*

By Easter morning, less than 12 hours after training ended, I climbed into my car. I smelled unwashed clothes and a rotted bean burrito. And I was still filthy. I couldn't pretend the smell of sweat and bad breath came from anyone but me.

My stomach churned with nerves as I merged onto the I-5 South. Focusing on the road ahead, I took deep breaths, imagining myself standing on the starting blocks of a swim race, waiting for the gun to go off. I slept hard, exhausted from lifeguard training, and had no time to figure out a strategy to handle my first day of work as a lifeguard. My car radio, tuned to KHJ's Boss Radio played, *Baby Come Back*. I tried to sing along, but the music scattered my thoughts and soon annoyed me, so I turned it off and drove in silence.

Carl told me that Calafia Street was the last freeway exit in San Clemente. A sign on the left read "San Clemente State Beach." It was 7:30 a.m. I was an hour and a half early. No one was at the entrance station, so I passed through and began circling a campground. I wasn't sure this was the right place, but I kept driving slowly, weaving between tents and RVs.

A tall, white tower structure caught my eye, perched on a high bluff with an expansive view overlooking the ocean. I parked next to the tower. A brown sign on the door read, "For Employees Only." Stepping out of my car, the morning was gray and overcast, but the scent of salty air and moisture felt refreshing. Far to my right, I could make out a pier, while the beach stretched empty to my left, curving around a point until it disappeared. Uncertainty and excitement met me at the same time.

With over an hour to wait, I examined my makeshift uniform: a plain white Hanes T-shirt and a red swimsuit I'd bought at JCPenney in Huntington Beach the night before. The swimsuit's knit material, complete with a liner, contradicted my vision for my first day of work. It was a V-neck, more of a fashion statement, drawing attention to my breasts instead of my position as a lifeguard. I had wanted a suit designed to showcase a lean, mean swimming machine. Instead, on this crucial first day, I felt lumpy with overexposed cleavage. I knew I needed to get a functional suit as soon as possible. Without red shorts, I wore Saddleback Gaucho swim-team sweatpants.

*This is not a good start.*

As I considered driving around some more, a yellow jeep approached with Carl driving. He pulled up next to me and smiled.

"Good morning," he said. "Let me show you how this works. Follow me, and I'll show you where to park."

I jumped back into my Dodge Colt, hoping it would start. It had a habit of going dead for no apparent reason. Thankfully, the engine turned over, and I followed Carl through the campground to a fenced area of white-stucco buildings. There were yellow jeeps, green trucks, and a long white building that reminded me of the Huntington office where I had interviewed for this job. Carl pointed out where to park. As I joined him, he greeted me again and said, "Welcome."

Relief washed over me, and I wondered where this smiling man had been during training when the instructors' smiles were reserved for moments when they laughed at us. Throughout that time, Carl and the other teachers seemed to loom over me, their presence large. But now, standing face to face, I realized Carl and I were the same size.

He walked me over to "The Shop," explaining that it was where lifeguards kept vehicles, equipment, and gear. He disappeared into the dark garage and returned with fins, binoculars, and a faded blue lifeguard jacket.

"You did well in training, Debbie. You came in sixth place overall," he said.

I smiled, pleased and surprised with my finish and Carl's approval.

I loaded my gear into his lifeguard jeep, and he drove us to the top of a trail in the campground. He navigated the vehicle down a steep, narrow path. I tried to keep my excitement in check, not wanting to appear too young or silly.

At the bottom of the trail, we went through a tunnel, passed under Amtrak railroad tracks, and emerged onto the sandy beach.

"This is Tower 1," Carl announced, pointing to our left.

It was a white lifeguard tower on a high, round concrete pedestal, marked with a large red number one painted on the front. I climbed the ladder with no rails, trying to keep my cool while pulling my gear up the uneven rungs. Carl climbed up and joined me. On the deck, we bumped into each other in the cramped space as we unbolted and removed the heavy plywood panels protecting the windows.

Inside the tower, the long red rescue tube lay draped across a flimsy director's chair. I grabbed it and wrapped the strap tight, setting it up for a clean, quick release—just like we'd practiced in training. I imagined heading to a rescue, pulling the loop, sliding the strap over my shoulder, the tube trailing behind me through the surf. I wanted to show Carl I had the basics down. He pointed to a nail hammered into the eave above the deck. I nodded and hung the tube in place.

The tour continued as Carl showed me the rest of the gear in the tower, including a red plastic first-aid kit the size of a shoe box and a black phone that provided a direct line to dispatch—my personal Bat Phone.

"Here's your 2316 key." He handed me a small, tarnished brass key. "It opens all the towers and most of the gates for Doheny, San Clemente, and San Onofre. Don't lose it," Carl's voice turned serious.

"Dispatch will help you with anything you need." He pointed to the white tower at the top of the bluff behind us—where I had parked early that morning. Then he climbed back down, waved, and drove away.

I was alone. My mind raced as I tried to visualize my notes from training. *What is a dispatcher?* Carl stressed that all I needed to do was pick up the handle on the phone and talk to the mysterious voice above.

I didn't fully comprehend his directions, but I did understand there was a person on the other end of the phone.

Carl left without any parting words of wisdom, and I panicked. My hands shook, and I walked back and forth on the small deck of the tower. I needed my list of procedures, but my training notes were in my car. I needed to shut my eyes to ground myself, but someone might drown if I did that. I did a big body shake, first my arms, then shoulders, legs, a couple of big hops, a final big breath in and out, and got myself together.

I could take a good test and swim a fast race, *but what exactly did a rescue look like?* In lifeguard training, we practiced rescues, but that's all it was—practice. I scanned the beach and my water for swimmers and any pending catastrophes.

Less than 24 hours after completing lifeguard training, I stood alone on an Easter Sunday in my tower. The beach and my water remained empty. I backed up, my attention locked on the water, and grabbed my borrowed pair of orange duck-feet fins and placed them on the tower deck. I set the binos on the front window ledge and practiced focusing them for the best close-up views. Scanning the beach and my water, I saw no swimmers. As I surveyed the coastline in both directions, the reality set in: I was the lifeguard on duty, solely responsible for this vast stretch of ocean, as far as I could see.

The black phone did not ring. I was usually not at a loss for words, but on this first day, silence was my default. I continued to stand, waiting for something to happen. It remained cold and overcast. I wrapped myself in the borrowed lifeguard jacket as a family emerged from the tunnel with two young boys wearing bright-orange inflatable water wings. During training, I learned that these flotation devices gave a false sense of safety and deflated quickly, making them more dangerous than helpful. I knew I must watch these two boys carefully. They would likely be my first rescues.

As the campground woke up and the children hunted their last Easter eggs, people began to stream through the tunnel, staking out spots in the sand near my tower. I looked to my right, at Tower 3, Calafia Street, and saw the tower open. The red tube hung vertically from the tower, announcing that another lifeguard was on duty. I had so many questions to ask and craved the company of another lifeguard. *I wish I could jog over and say hi.*

Eventually a jeep appeared from under the tunnel and parked in front of my tower. I learned it was Unit 4505, the call number for the San Clemente State Beach vehicle. Not wanting to look directly at the two men—so they wouldn't think I'd stopped watching my water—I used my peripheral vision. During training, the instructors had hammered into us the importance of never taking our eyes off the ocean, never turning our backs to it, and the life-and-death consequences of even a moment's lapse. I wanted them to see I was a good lifeguard.

The guard on the passenger side motioned at me to come to the unit. I wanted to tell them about the two boys wearing water wings, but I didn't see them. There were still no swimmers in the water.

*Where were my little boys? Did I not see them enter the water? Did they drown on my watch?*

An awful taste bubbled up in my mouth, and I felt like I might throw up. Tube and fins in hand, I descended the ladder, looking forward. When my feet hit the sand, I saw the water wings in a pile of the family's belongings. The boys were digging holes in the wet sand near the water's edge as their parents sat close and watched. Relieved, I approached the unit.

The unit guards introduced themselves and said they knew it was my first day.

The driver remarked, "It's cold, and there's not much of a swell; it might be a quiet day. Do you want a break? Would you like to jump in the water?"

I didn't want to jump in the water on that cold day, but their offer felt like a quiet directive. I kept my mouth shut, nodding yes instead. Asking questions, I feared, would expose my inexperience.

I stripped down into my awful red swimsuit.

"Do I need my tube?" I asked.

"No, just go in," he replied.

Trying to look casual, I jogged toward the water and felt a rush of self-consciousness, wondering if they were looking at my butt. Slowly, I entered the ocean, felt the sandy bottom, and dove under a small wave. My stress dissipated, and I melted. Relief washed over me, and my mind settled. I was alone in the water. Everything was quiet, and in that moment, I felt safe.

Returning to the unit, I walked backward, watching my people-less water. My towel was up in the tower, and

I felt awkward during this reunion with the unit guards. I stood next to them, soaking wet, in my stupid V-neck suit that clung in all the wrong places. They sat relaxed in their uniforms, wide-brimmed straw hats and Ray-Ban sunglasses, their Rainbow sandals perched casually on the unit's dashboard.

"Call dispatch if you need anything and stay alert," they said, and drove away.

Back in my tower, as I dried off, the phone rang. I stepped backward, still watching the water. "Tower 1," I answered.

"Debbie, this is Tim Harvey, your dispatcher for the day. Do you see the people to the left of your tower? Tell them they need to put their dogs on a leash. Leave the phone off the hook and hang it up when you're back in your tower."

I followed Tim's instructions precisely.

"Excuse me, sir, you must put these dogs on leashes. It's a state park rule." I expected the guy to laugh at me—a woman in a swimsuit carrying fins and a rescue tube, telling him what to do. Instead, relief as the man complied, pulled out leashes, and followed my request.

It was 1 p.m., and the sun had finally begun to break through the clouds, coaxing a few people to wade into the water up to their knees. Soon after, a woman ran up to my tower.

She cried out, "My husband cut his foot and needs help!"

She pointed to a man sitting in the sand to my right. I picked up my phone and told dispatch, "I am responding to a report of an injured man about 25 yards to my right." To help me judge distances, I imagined them as swimming pools, both a 25-yard short course and a 50-meter long course.

With my fins, tube, and first-aid kit, I ran down the beach to my first-ever first aid. The injured man was on his back, spread out in the sand, with his injured foot in the air. He was old, maybe in his 40s, with black hair, pale skin, and lots of dark chest hair. A thumb-sized piece of jagged glass stuck in and out of the heel of his left foot. I told him to stay calm and gently held his foot.

There was some blood, and it trickled onto my hand, but not enough to trigger a tourniquet response. I stared at him, then at his foot, unsure of what to do.

He kept saying, "How bad is it? Take it out, please."

I didn't think I was supposed to pull the glass out, but he couldn't walk away to go to a doctor. I scanned my water and wondered how I could simultaneously watch my water and the man's foot. As I contemplated my options, the unit pulled up beside us. The guards quickly assessed the man's vitals, pulse, and respirations.

"You can return to your tower, Debbie. We'll stabilize his foot. He needs to go to a doctor to have the glass removed."

The wind was picking up, and people were packing their gear and making a slow exodus up the trail. I was still standing on the deck outside the tower, too scared to sit. The stress from a week of intense training and today, my first day on the job, weighed on me. *Stay alert*, I told myself.

Then, the phone rang, and my dispatcher, Tim, said, "Do you see the man in the water to your right?"

I had been watching the man Tim pointed out, and he

appeared safe. I saw no rip current, and the man looked comfortable in the water. He was not attempting to return to shore, and I assumed he was fine. Tim added urgency to his voice. "That's a rescue! Go!"

I grabbed my tube and fins and blazed down the ladder, sprinting to my right, trying to figure out why I had to rescue this man. I entered the water and quickly realized I was on sharp, jagged rocks, and so was he. The rocks were too sharp to run over, so I lay flat on my belly and dragged my tube behind me. There was no grand entrance into the water. Instead, I looked like a beached sea lion humping my way back to sea.

Gently, I rolled over, trying to stay as flat as possible. I put my fins on and made little dolphin kicks, mini-undulations, toward him. There was little surf, and I reached the man quickly by pulling myself over the reef on my stomach.

"I'm a lifeguard, and I'm going to help you," I told him.

He allowed me to wrap and secure the tube around his torso. The water was not deep, and I squatted, bent my knees, and pushed us up and off the rocks like a backstroke start in a pool. The fins on my feet protected me from the sharp rocks and allowed me to extend my legs as I repeated this until we were clear of the danger zone. With clear, sandy-bottomed water, I pulled him to shore. He appeared to be okay, and I saw no blood pouring out from either of us. I asked his name and where he was from for my rescue card and ran back to my tower.

I hung up the tower phone to alert dispatch I'd returned, and it rang back at me immediately. Tim told me I'd just made a "rock" rescue. It wasn't just a rock sitting in the water, he explained, but a reef about the size of a 25-yard pool, visible only at certain low tides. I learned that Tower 1 was responsible for making early safety contacts to keep people away from that danger zone.

As I examined the razor-thin cuts on my hands, I wondered why no one had told me about the rock earlier.


Everything I faced during my first day on the job was different from what I learned in lifeguard training. I looked up and down the beach and tried to establish some connections. I saw the pier, Tower 3, the tunnel, and the point vanishing on the other side, the hidden rock, and my phone—the link to dispatch. I had so much to learn.

I didn't even know how I would find my car after work.

Tim called. "Debbie, congrats on your first day. It's time to close up."

The heavy plywood window covers were tough to figure out as I stood on the narrow deck high above the ground. As I struggled with the splintered plywood, a jeep pulled up, and a lifeguard offered to help. I hesitated, wondering if it was a kind offer or if it was because I was a woman.

Nick Sopha introduced himself with a friendly grin and told me the window covers were difficult for all the guards. He climbed into the tower and helped me lift the heavy wood into the runners that held it in place. We worked together to secure the rusty nuts and bolts that kept people from breaking into the towers.

Once the tower was locked, Nick offered me a ride up the trail and said, "There will be a rookie orientation sometime in May. We try to schedule new lifeguards with full-time work Memorial Day through Labor Day."

May seemed far off, and I counted the months that would pass while I swam and went to school.

*What was the rush to have me work today, the day after I finished lifeguard training?*

As Nick dropped me off at my car, he asked, "What does it feel like to be the first woman lifeguard at San Clemente State Beach?"

I was a scared rookie and didn't think about being a woman. I was unsure about my skills and worried about keeping everyone safe on my beach.

I paused. "I don't know yet, Nick."

I waved goodbye, sat in my car, and put my hat over my head to think about the past week. My stomach ended the silence, and I went in search of some burritos. Then I needed to find a phone to call Kim. She was at San Diego State and would start lifeguard training in three weeks. I was desperate to tell her everything.

$$6$$

# *Mermaids*

## *Queen Diana*

It didn't surprise me that Laguna Beach was home to mermaids. If I stood still and quiet, gazing out at the ocean from Main Beach, I'd see a splash, then another, until a pod of mermaids emerged. They laughed and frolicked before diving in unison, their glistening flukes slicing through the air before vanishing beneath the waves.

In the summer of 1972, 15 girls under 12 years old transformed into Mermaids, following their Queen Diana Slowski into the waters of Laguna Beach. Diana turned the beaches of Laguna into one giant aquatic playground. She ran and danced with her Mermaids, leading them into the water to swim and explore offshore reefs. She encouraged them to open their eyes underwater and look at the bright-orange Garibaldi weaving through the kelp. The fish were unafraid and looked back at the Mermaids like they were long-lost relatives.

Diana led them to hidden pocket beaches. "Follow me," she said, taking them out into the waves and teaching them how to bodysurf—a skill every Mermaid must master.

Laguna Beach had always held a special place in my heart. In those early summers, before I knew the coastline well, I'd drive north from Doheny and Dana Point Harbor, my mind crossing into an imaginary land I called the Island of Laguna. My pulse fluttered as sandy beaches gave way to rocky coves and offshore reefs. Each time, I became an explorer, sailing toward a foreign shore and embarking into a new and different land.

Pacific Coast Highway took me past shops selling tie-dye sarongs, bikinis, veggie burritos, and smoothies. The air was thick with incense and patchouli oil. Art was everywhere—hanging in galleries and spread out on sidewalks, where painters with easels crafted their masterpieces.

Cave-like bookshops dotted the main street. I bought my first copy of *The Color Purple* and other mind-altering books, like *The Great Railway Bazaar* and Hunter S. Thompson's gonzo writings. Laguna was a place to expand my horizons.

The main beach at Laguna was the heart of the city, marked by its iconic white medieval-style lifeguard head-quarters. At the base of the tower, the Mermaids gathered on dry sand to start their summer days.

Like Homer's Sirens, these young girls were drawn to the sea, even when the world tried to tell them otherwise. At a time when Junior Lifeguard programs excluded girls, Diana led her Mermaids, free from rules and limitations, challenging them to thrive in the ocean.

As the summer days blended, Diana decided that her Mermaids were strong enough to experience the famous "Woods Cove Blowhole." Millennia of water created this natural wonder, opening a narrow tunnel into the rocky coastal cliffs and allowing waves to surge through and burst upward in a dramatic spray of water and mist.

The Blowhole attracted visitors and photographers, its rocks slick with mist and waves surging in and out. One minute, an innocent bystander leaned in for a closer look, the water rushing back and forth beneath him. The next, a surge exploded upward, spraying his face. He slipped on the wet rock and slid straight into the Blowhole, screaming, "Help me!" In an instant, the spectator became a rescue. Moments later, a lifeguard jumped in, pulled him out of the water—shaken, but unhurt.

Diana told Lifeguard Chief Bruce Baird about her plans. Bruce walked her around the lifeguard headquarters, glancing back and forth to ensure privacy, and told her, "This is too much for the girls."

Diana nodded, feigned compliance, and went ahead with her plan to take her Mermaids through the washing machine—the churning fury and power inside the Blowhole.

The girls stepped forward, drawn to the enormous whoosh. A young Mermaid named Shelly looked down about 10 feet and watched as a powerful jet of water shot through the hole with an earth-shaking boom. The Woods Cove Blowhole never stopped; it was an endless cycle of fury and power. Shelly nervously looked up at Diana and waited for her instructions. Diana reached for Shelly's hand and squeezed it tightly.

"First, I time the incoming swell that fills this bowl," Diana said, pointing to the low area between the rocks. She stood with confidence. Shelly and the other Mermaids were rapt as she continued, "Pay attention. Watch how the hole fills." She paused and pointed again. "Now the water is pulling out."

She demonstrated how to hold their breath—a simple skill but one quickly forgotten when leaping into churning water.

Diana waited for the incoming swell and jumped. She vanished down into the foamy, churning water, and the girls held their breath. Just as Diana predicted, she was flushed through the water and pulled out of the bowl with the surge of thick water, beyond the jagged rocks. From outside the rocks, she waved to her girls.

The Mermaids clapped and screamed for their Queen.

Diana climbed out of the water and returned to her girls. One by one, she timed their entry, said, "Now," and watched them leap—trusting her completely, meeting the challenge with courage that would serve each Mermaid her entire life.

For Mermaid Ingrid, it was only the beginning.

# Ingrid

Ingrid Loos and Bruce Baird were standing in knee-high water on Catalina Island as they held the 16-foot white dory with its narrow bow facing east, twenty-two miles across the Catalina Channel to their final destination: Ports O'Call, Los Angeles. It was 1982, and Ingrid had been a Laguna Beach lifeguard for six summers.

This was the third time Ingrid and Bruce had competed in the Catalina Dory Race to the mainland. Dories were not part of modern guarding. But they were enduring symbols of a time when lifeguards braved the surf. The boats were holdovers from the mid-1800s and early 1900s, when surfmen on the Atlantic coast rowed out to shipwrecks to save sailors' lives. The tradition of rowing dories remained strong, with California lifeguards in many agencies still using them for training and competition.

Twenty dories lined up on both sides of Ingrid's and Bruce's boat. Their crews adjusted oars, secured their gear, and stretched quietly.

The sky was clear, the ocean glassy, the air temperature in the mid-60s. Perfect rowing weather. But every team knew how fast conditions could change.

*Never underestimate the ocean*, Ingrid reminded herself.

She pressed herself up and over the gunwale of the dory and sat on the bench closest to the bow. Grabbing her oars, she secured them in the locks on each side. Ingrid faced shore, put both oar blades in the water, and steadied the boat for Bruce. She took a slow breath and reminded herself that she'd done this row before.

*I can do this.*

Bruce hooked his right leg over the side of the dory, hoisted himself up and over with his arms, and flopped into the boat. Ingrid shook her head and knew what came next.

"Arghhh," he cried as Ingrid watched him take a direct thump to his groin.

Once in the boat, he pulled himself onto his seat, grabbed his oars, and said, "Let's go."

Bruce set the pace, his feet planted hard on the flat bottom of the dory. He leaned back, pulling the oars to his chest and the blades deep enough, but not too deep in the water to get full momentum. Ingrid sat on the bench behind Bruce and matched every stroke precisely, with both grace and power. They did not verbalize the process; they rowed together intuitively, facing Catalina, their backs to their finish line.

Both wore pantyhose under their shorts to prevent painful rub marks on their skin from the stationary wooden benches they would sit on to make the crossing. They brought Erg, a pre-Gatorade electrolyte replacement, to stay hydrated during the six to seven hour row.

I had tried rowing the Pendleton dory with Scott a few times: splinters, grease, waves over the bow. It was not my idea of fun, and I wanted out of the boat. It made me admire Ingrid's quiet determination even more.

Decades later, as I talked with Ingrid, now in her late 60s, I was struck by her passion for rowing. The Catalina dory crossing wasn't just a race. It was a test of endurance and teamwork, with two people having no choice but to keep going.

"Bruce brought a poncho. He thought of everything," Ingrid laughed.

I imagined rowing a dory, stroke after stroke, hour after hour, and thinking, *Oh, no. I need to poop.* As your partner tried to row alone, waves and water crashing against and into the dory, you crawled into the poncho, pulled down your shorts and pantyhose, leaned your ass over the side, and let loose.

"Thankfully, I never had to go," Ingrid said.

Laguna kept its dory chained to the Main Beach Lifeguard Headquarters, where Bruce and Ingrid became regulars—pushing and pulling the dory down to the surf and rowing out to sea, during years when women rarely lifeguarded, let alone rowed dories.

Ingrid knew she'd been allowed into an elite club. Her mentor, Bruce, never let her forget it.

In the small, tight community of Laguna Beach in the 1970s and 1980s, the postman, school-bus driver, and mayor all watched Ingrid and Bruce train and compete over the years. Around town, they were known as "the Old Man and the Girl."

When I returned to Laguna in the spring of 2025, memories of my early pilgrimages there as a young lifeguard flooded back. I stood in front of lifeguard headquarters, watching dolphins swim close to shore. To my right, I looked at a mural, prominent on Main Beach—a large painting of the ocean and a dory team in the surf, a man and a woman rowing out to sea. There were no names, no plaque, no caption.

But I knew. Decades later, they were the Old Man and the Girl.

Long before that mural existed, Ingrid and Bruce were preparing for the Catalina Dory Race. There were no hotels in the Isthmus of Catalina, the starting point for the race, and like the other teams, Ingrid and Bruce spent the night on the beach with the other competitors. Ingrid saw other teams sleep under the stars in sleeping bags, some with blankets and others in little pup tents.

At bedtime, she and Bruce took a tarp and created a lean-to. Ingrid held the blue-plastic tarp and attached one end to the high side of the dory. Bruce crawled on the sandy ground and found stones to secure the base.

Bruce entered the tent first, and Ingrid watched. Then she scooched into the tent feet first. Bruce slept with Ingrid's feet, and she slept with his—the "head-to-toe" position, a flimsy illusion of boundaries.

For Ingrid, it didn't erase the awkwardness. This was their third time sleeping on the beach together, and still her stomach ached, her head pounded, and a queasy unease settled in—the same unease that never entirely left, not after three races, and not after years of whatever it was with Bruce.

Out of the lean-to, they professed their total trust in each other, as all good dory partners did. In the open ocean, the weather can become treacherous, dories can flip, partners can get sick, and your life is literally in each other's hands. Like good relationships, good partners are vulnerable to the best and worst in each other.

She knew she could walk away from Bruce on land, but there was no escape in a dory out at sea.

"The relationship was so, so complicated," Ingrid shared years later.

As they rowed, their backs to the finish line, the Catalina shoreline shrank. Bruce had mounted a compass on the stern to chart the course he could not see.

Ingrid wrote about the crossings for the Laguna Beach historical records:

> *"The channel was an intense, deep, dark blue. We saw sharks sunning themselves on the surface and flying fish skipping about. It felt like a big ocean, threatening and immense."*

Long before the Catalina crossing, Ingrid's path had started at Main Beach as a Laguna Beach Mermaid with Diana. During summer breaks, she inhaled a big bowl of Sugar Pops and rushed to the beach for her job as a beach rat— bodysurfing, swimming, and running. At dusk, she clocked out, sunburned and salty, and went home to her sandy bedsheets, ready to do it all over again.

Chief Bruce Baird watched Ingrid grow up on the beach, and, in 1976, when she was 15, he approached her wearing only his red swim trunks. She was much taller than Bruce, but she felt small and shy, wondering what she had done to garner the Chief's attention. He pointed to the shady side of the Main Beach Lifeguard headquarters, and she followed Bruce slowly, obediently, and step by step in the soft, hot sand. *What does he want with me? Did I do something wrong?* Ingrid wondered.

They stopped, and Bruce put his hands on his hips and looked up at Ingrid's face. "Would you like to be a lifeguard?" he asked.

*Me?* Ingrid looked around to confirm he was talking to her. The lifeguards she watched were older and all men.

Still too young to drive or sign legal papers, Ingrid told her parents, "I need you to come sign some papers at the beach."

At lifeguard headquarters, Ingrid, her parents, and Bruce squeezed into a narrow space between a foot wash sink, a first-aid cabinet, and the spiral stairs leading to dispatch above. Bruce looked up at Ingrid, fifteen years old and pushing 6 feet tall, and said, "I'm personally in charge of you and your training."

Her parents nodded. No questions, no hesitation. From that day on, she called him "Daddy Bruce."

As I listened to her story, I wondered, too. Would I have questioned this if it were my daughter? My kids grew up as Junior Lifeguards, and I knew they were capable. Could they handle the weight of life-and-death decisions at 15? Would I have been concerned about the man in charge?

I wasn't sure.

Ingrid trained with senior lifeguards, and, when she turned 16, Bruce gave her the A-OK to work alone. There was no ceremony, no announcement, just his permission. In 1976, Ingrid became Laguna's first woman lifeguard and worked alongside 65 men.

She stood with the guards before the Main Beach headquarters, wearing her red one-piece uniform. At 6 feet tall, Ingrid stood eye-to-eye with the guards. But she hunched her shoulders and crossed her arms over her chest to stay incognito.

The men around her were comfortable in their teeny, tiny Hind Wells trunks, at ease in their bodies, or at least pretended to be. They stood beside her, poking and prodding each other. Ingrid stayed quiet and looked out at the ocean. They weren't talking about the dangerous shorebreak developing below the berm.

"She's a 6," one guard said, pointing at a brunette in a bright blue bikini. They gave every woman a number—thin, fat, pretty, ugly. If a woman made them jump up and thrust their hips, she was a 10.

Ingrid swallowed. *Were they rating her, too?*

Ingrid had a front-row seat to the not-so-secret lives of the men she worked with—raw, unfiltered, unashamed. And where was Daddy Bruce?

He became her boss, mentor, and, in some ways, a father figure. She gave Bruce her obedience and a nervous giggle.

During her first summer, Ingrid arrived at a foggy, deserted Main Beach at 7 a.m., just as Bruce instructed.

He appeared disheveled and unshaven, in a coffee-stained T-shirt. He looked as if he had slept on the beach.

"Today we do in-and-outs," he said. "Sprint into the water, swim past the surf line, and swim back. On shore, I want 25 push-ups and 25 jumping jacks. Repeat ten times."

He said it was training to make her stronger. He believed in her, and Ingrid did the workout, believing him back.

But Bruce's attention wasn't just on her performance—he obsessed over her body. He tracked her weight like it was part of the job, jotting down numbers and making comments as if he were doing her a favor.

"Your thighs are winking back at me," or "You've got quite a secretarial spread."

On Catalina, when they slept head to toe, he kept his mouth shut. But back in Laguna, he went right back to it— telling her how fat her butt looked while she slept.

"I was never safe from ridicule, even during my sleep," Ingrid told me. I laughed along. What else was there to do?"

Decades later, she reflected on Bruce. "He was my boss and friend, and everything became confusing. We rowed across the Catalina Channel together three times. He helped me get my Emergency Medical Technician certificate. But it wasn't until I was in my 40s that I fully understood how *wrong* it was. Bruce was much older, and he held the power and esteem."

Ingrid rose through the ranks. She became a lifeguard supervisor. As a woman once judged like a bikini contestant, she now provided leadership and guidance from the jeep.

She supported young guards without the scrutiny, ridicule, and the double standards she had endured.

Her path went beyond lifeguarding. Today, Ingrid is a successful businesswoman and athlete and owns the Fearless Endurance Triathlon Club and Coaching, in Irvine.

One rescue in particular stayed with her:

*"One evening, Karen Koster and I were the only two guards handling the late shift, driving around in the jeep, when a call came in: Crescent Bay.*

*A man, strung out on drugs, was running wild. We called the police, but he took off, bolting up an embankment and over a chain-link fence.*

*The cop tried to follow, but his gun belt got caught in the fence. I didn't wait. I jumped the fence, chased the guy down, and tackled him. We tumbled down the hill, all the way back to the sand. The cop finally caught up and sprayed Mace on both of us. The crowd cheered. I couldn't see a thing. But I knew I had passed the test."*

Ingrid had once followed her Mermaid Queen, Diana, through the Blowhole, a tunnel of crashing water, trusting she'd come out the other side. She did. Years later, she was the one others trusted to lead and save lives.

Pendleton Coast Lifeguards, 1979

7

# *Pendleton*

*The idea of female ocean lifeguards in the '70s was, to put it mildly, revolutionary to many lifeguards of that era, and in 1978, it finally happened. Two women had tested to be lifeguards at San Clemente and had successfully passed training.*

*We fretted about the slipping of standards, the potential for problems in the locker room, and that we would have to alter our sometimes sexist, sophomoric, and profane banter in response to their presence. It was the end of the world as we knew it, and we were fairly certain that they wouldn't measure up. That lasted about as long as it took for us to realize that every one of them could swim circles around 90% of the men on staff at that time.*

--Mike Brousard, Pendleton Coast Lifeguard,
1970 - 2013

*Is this the locker room? This place stinks.*

I looked into the dark space called "The Shop" and covered my mouth and nose. The air reeked of motor oil, sweat, and stale beer—and something greasy and feral, like a dead rat rotting somewhere. My body tensed. I lowered my head, stepped into a room built for men, and tried not to swallow the smell.

It took a moment for my eyes to adjust to the darkness. A small, grimy window in the back let in a dust-filled shaft of hazy sun. A torn vinyl bench seat, maybe from a car, was wedged underneath the window. Weights lay scattered across the floor, and a black punching bag swung from the open-framed ceiling. Crumpled cans of Coors spilled out of a dented metal trash can, and I remembered how much I hated the smell of spilled beer.

To my left, a yellow lifeguard jeep sat with its hood up and its engine exposed.


Rookie orientation started a few days before Memorial Day 1978. I'd worked Easter Sunday, then heard nothing for two months—no call to return—until this day. At the time, I didn't know getting work was unusual for a rookie. The older guards usually grabbed every open shift for the extra hours and money. Later, when Carl and I became friends, I learned why I'd been called in to work the day after training finished: I was the new girl.

Kim and I stood in the maintenance yard with 12 other new lifeguards to get our marching orders. We were the first women hired to lifeguard Doheny, San Clemente, and San Onofre State Beaches—the Pendleton Coast.

One of the supervisors, Mike Brousard, a big, muscular, older guy, maybe in his late 20s, his biceps pushing against the seams of his uniform shirt, told us, "We post the schedule twice a month on the bulletin board in the shop. We will try to give you 40 hours a week through Labor Day, but there are no guarantees."

He kept his face serious, his voice low and calm. "There are no shift trades; we place you in specific towers to gain experience."

I made a mental note: *don't piss this guy off.*

We walked to the shop in a tight pack, trying to look cool and casual. But instead, we looked like a pack of newly hatched ducklings, bumping into each other, wobbling in the tight space as we searched for our mom, any mom.

I squeezed between the other rookies and pushed myself to the front row to see the schedule. I found my name on the list and wrote down the days and numbers I didn't understand—T12 and SS4.

Kim stood outside the garage, waiting for me. With our schedules in hand, we walked toward our cars through a gauntlet of mostly good-looking men. We leaned against the trunk of Kim's yellow Ford Capri and laughed, a combination of relief and fear.

"What are we doing here?" Kim looked at me and shook her head.

Kim had finished lifeguard training a few weeks after me, and between her at San Diego State and me at Saddleback, there was a lot of territory to cover. Boyfriends, sex, swimming, and the minutiae of everything said during today's meeting.

But first: "Do you know where the bathroom is?"

Kim pointed to the maintenance building in front of the shop. "There's a toilet over there, but I'd hold it if I were you."

Carl was my go-to face in the crowd, and I watched him walk over to us.

I moved too close to him and pushed my notes in his face, anxious for answers. T12? SS4? "What does all this mean?"

Carl grinned. "T12 is Doheny, with a start time of 10 a.m. Go to dispatch, and he'll show you the times and location for each shift. And, by the way, both of you should keep some extra clothes with you for after work." He rattled off a list, "Olamendi's, workouts, parties, and Santa Inez. Just come hang out. There's always something going on."

Kim and I did the nervous giggle, the default reaction around men when we didn't know what to say. We wanted in, whatever "in" was.

"Let's make a list of stuff we should pack," I said.

Kim pushed my shoulder. "You're so anal retentive."

I gave her a dirty look. "What does that even mean?"

At the park entrance, prepared to work my first Doheny day, I told the kiosk guy I was a lifeguard. He let out a dramatic sigh, like I was trying to sneak in for free. I reached for my fins and thought they would serve as proof of identity, but instead, he waved me through: "You're holding up traffic."

Cigarette butts, potato-chip bags, and black bonfire scars

littered my path to Tower 12. As I dragged gear through the sand, dust and grit marked my footprints. This wasn't San Clemente's golden sand and blue, dolphin-laden water.

I unlocked the door to my tower and tried to orient myself to this new beach.

As I stood on the deck, the San Juan Creek to my left divided Doheny in half. A stone's throw to my right was a rock jetty that served as the downcoast entrance to the Dana Point Harbor.

I watched sailboats and fishing vessels motor in and out of the harbor. Surfers arrived with their longboards, walked past my tower, and paddled out alongside the rock jetty.

With my tower open and my gear in place, a yellow jeep rolled up next to me: the unit. At Doheny, it was called "4506." It patrolled the beach, gave breaks, and backed up rescues.

Dave Perry, also known as DP, was one of my supervisors. He greeted me with a smile and a broad, open-armed gesture. He clapped his hands together, rubbing them back and forth like a genie with a magic lantern. His kind demeanor made me forget my rookie fears, and for a moment, I believed everything might be wonderful, maybe even fun.

Bob Bonebrake sat in the passenger seat, the "shotgun" position. He was well over 6 feet tall, with dark hair and a large, long face. He was fit, but there was something unswimmer-like about him. *Maybe he was a water-polo guy.*

"Call me Boner," he said.

*Boner, huh? Does everyone here have a nickname? And does Boner mean what I think it does?* I glanced down at his small

Dolphin shorts and then caught myself.

*Jeez, quit looking!* I panicked and looked out at the ocean and hoped he hadn't noticed.

Dave climbed into my tower and pointed at the surfers. He explained that the waves formed when swells pushed and refracted off the rocky jetty. "We call it Boneyard because of the sharp reef rocks hidden beneath the water's surface. There's a fixed rip along the jetty where most of the surfers paddle out."

*So, Boner and Boneyard?* I didn't look at Bob's shorts this time.

Boner smiled a big, mischievous grin, pointed to the massive headland beyond the harbor, and yelled at Dave, "Tell her about Killer Dana."

"4506, respond to Tower 8." Quickly, my lesson and their visit were over. Dave climbed down the ladder. Bob, Boner, or whatever I was supposed to call him, moved to the driver's seat, turned on the red lights, and beeped the siren.

Dave ran to the front of the unit, dropped to his hands and knees to look for anyone hidden underneath, yelled, "Clear!" and jumped in as they sped away.

They were gone. I was alone again, and wondered what the emergency was.

Determined that nobody would drown in my water, I watched for swimmers, toddlers, or anyone who intended to enter the Boneyard. I ran back and forth, keeping the swimmers and surfers apart from each other, and looked for anyone walking toward me with bloody feet.

It was a confusing day. I called Station 30, the Doheny

HQ, every time a boat came close to the jetty, which was all the time given this was the mouth of the harbor. The dispatcher was patient and gave me pointers to identify boats in the wrong position or sails flapping without wind. I made no rescues, which concerned me because I thought at least a dozen people would have thanked me for saving their lives by my second day.

Instead, I sat squirming in the tower. Leakage was imminent. I crossed my legs tightly and hoped I could wait it out. *Do I call Dispatch?* Finally, 4506 pulled up beside my tower.

"Dave, I need to pee." I cringed, humiliated.

He climbed into my tower to watch my water and pointed to the picnic-area bathroom.

With my towel around my waist, I jogged and waddled over. *Just hang on for one more minute.*


After our shifts, Kim and I raced around to find each other. We met at Señor Pedros on El Camino.

Kim started: "I worked Tower 1, San Clemente. I didn't have any rock rescues like you warned me about, but I made three rescues!"

Kim shared every detail with me: calling in the rescue, her swims out through the surf, the size and direction of the swell, clipping the victims in, and swimming them back to shore.

"It was so exciting. This big guy was in a rip right in front of my tower. He was crying and did everything I told him to do. I pulled him in just like training."

Jealousy invaded my thoughts. I'd only had the one rock rescue—the Marine on my first day, back in March—and I was pretty sure I'd messed that one up. Regardless, I let it go and focused on Kim. I needed to memorize everything she said.

We carefully analyzed every detail of her rescues.

"Did the unit guards say anything? Compliments or blow-its?" I begged her to tell me everything. "Let's go over the whole thing one more time."

Getting hired with Kim, rather than working as the lone first woman, meant I wasn't alone. We bounced our fears off each other, confessed our mistakes, and hashed out every detail until there was nothing left to say. No topic was off limits. We vented, confided, and unloaded. Whatever had gnawed at me during the day, I let it go after talking with Kim. My mind stopped the endless spinning over what I'd done right or wrong, and I slept hard and deep at night.

As those early tower days passed, Kim and I shared our swimsuit problems, such as sand making a permanent home between our legs. There were days it looked like I wore a diaper under my suit. And always, I kept my eyes on the water and tried not to let the other guards know about my sandy problem.

There were makeshift solutions, and I showed Kim how to cut the inside liner in her suit so that the sand could escape.

"And the Marines at Tower 3, Calafia?" Kim said. We both had problems getting those young, macho boys to take the rescue tube from a woman.

"I didn't want the unit guards to think I couldn't handle it."

"Me, too," Kim nodded.

We talked about the new lifeguards we met, all men, every time we turned around. Who was helpful? Was he handsome? Did he raise his eyebrows or give you side-eyes? Did he laugh with you or at you? We both agreed that Dave, DP, was someone we could trust with our most basic questions.

I told Kim about John Mulvana, also known as Mulva, one of our bosses. He had stood in front of the shop, his hands on hips, and, in front of everyone in earshot, looked at me, smiled, and barked, "We'll see if you can cut it."

I faked confidence, but underneath I was terrified of making mistakes, or worse, someone drowning. Even on quiet, misty mornings with no one on the beach, my pulse raced and my legs felt unsteady. I wasn't sure I could cut it.

New towers, different beaches, rescues, and my first summer rolled forward.

And then, when I least expected it, I fell in love with lifeguarding.

Maybe it was an August tidal event, but I felt the shift. I woke with the sun and threw the sandy sheets off my body. No slow wake-up. Just big, loud steps through the apartment, grabbing gear, brushing my teeth if there was time. My only focus: get to the beach.

At night, I drifted to sleep, excited for the next day, ready to face the fear, the thrill, the all-consuming addiction of another day as an ocean lifeguard.

My senses were on overdrive, the ocean tasted saltier, and the surf pounded in my chest. A simple jog on the beach turned into a movie reel of everything that could happen and how I'd respond.

It was still exhausting. But as I learned more, my mind quieted. The fear didn't disappear. But I found moments of calm, a deep sense that I had found my calling, and the job became exciting.

From Tower 5 in San Clemente, I enjoyed this moment of Zen, my 18-year-old version of enlightenment, when the unit pulled up. I saw them coming, but I didn't do the cool sunglasses-on-my-nose nod. I watched a young girl, maybe eight, without fins on a boogie board, flailing in shallow water. I didn't think she was a rescue, but when the unit drove closer, I started to doubt myself. My savvy lessons about observation and unspoken body-language shit fell apart.

I put my hand on my rescue tube. Looked at the girl. Looked at the unit, and decided to make a rescue. I threw the phone off the hook, ran down in front of the unit, jumped into knee-deep water, and pulled her to shore.

The unit waited until I was back in my tower and then continued down the beach without saying a word. *Maybe I did the right thing?*

Rock swims became part of my mornings before work. I ran down the San Clemente trail in my swimsuit, holding a pair of goggles. Kim and Scott waited for me and were ready to swim. The morning was gray and overcast. A few surfers sat outside the rock, hoping for waves to materialize. Scott nodded, and we jogged down the beach.

While nothing was routine this first rookie summer—filled with new towers, beaches, and constantly changing conditions—these morning workouts became a quiet ritual. I jogged on the empty beach, past closed towers, and looked at the ocean with excitement.

At Tower 4 (locals called it Riviera), Kim, Scott, and I looked at Seal Rock, about 600 yards offshore. The reef was visible, but the horizon was blurry in the overcast sky.

"Fucking weather," Scott muttered.

I leaned toward Kim and whispered, "Do you ever think about sharks?"

She threw her arms in the air, shook her head, and laughed. "Remember *Jaws*? The fisher guy sliding down the deck, straight into the great white shark's mouth?"

We smiled, even Scott. Talking about sharks felt like bad juju.

Slowly, we entered the water. I tiptoed in, letting my body adjust to the assault. The anticipation of cold water was always worse than the reality, and after a few strokes, I forgot about the cold. We picked our lines to swim straight to the rock and started together.

I smelled the sea lions before I saw them. I turned my head to breathe, and a warm, rotting stink punched me in the face. I stopped swimming and went full drama queen—spitting, gagging, flailing—making sure Kim and Scott didn't miss a second of my suffering. As we neared the rock, the sea lions dove away from us, barking and slapping the water, annoyed by our intrusion.

We swam around to the back of the rock and used the swell to push us up onto handholds, climbing our version of Everest. The surface was jagged and slick, and we moved slowly. Reef cuts on my hands and feet were the price paid to stand atop the rock and declare victory. They didn't hurt at first, barely visible, like a papercut, but I kept an eye on the razor-sharp wounds that could get red, hot, and puffy within a few days.

Reef cuts and urinary-tract infections from sitting in hot, damp, sandy swimsuits became occupational hazards. Neosporin and unfiltered cranberry juice quickly became my new, essential friends.

One clear morning, as I swam the rock, I watched the sun filter through the thick kelp beds, where bright orange Garibaldi fish darted back and forth doing their laps. Maybe they were relatives of the Laguna Garibaldi that swam with the Mermaids?

We started the swim back separately. I jumped off the rock, ready to swim back to shore, when something caught my eye. With trepidation, I dove down into the kelp and saw a fish, big and scary compared to the small fish darting in and out of the reef and kelp forest. *What is that?*

It was about the size of my forearm, thick and blocky, with a body painted in bands of black and rust, white around the mouth, and it had lips! I came up for air, squealed, and pointed below. It was scary and beautiful. I wanted to give it space. This was not a fish found in the stuffed-animal section of toy stores.

I'd never seen anything like this on *The Undersea World of Jacques Cousteau*. I had a deep wish to discover, to be like Cousteau. Maybe I was the first person in the world to see this block fish?

Back on shore, I gave Scott a detailed account of my discovery, and he told me that the fish, a Sheepshead, was pretty common in the area. "Some of the lifeguards dive for them, and they're tasty eating."

On the other hand, Garibaldi held the designation as California's state fish, left alone by law to swim freely.

We jogged back to Tower 1 and went our separate ways. It was time to go to work.

After our shifts, Kim and I promised to meet at 106 Santa Inez. Carl had told Kim and me on our first day of orientation that Santa Inez was *the* place to go. Nick, the guard who helped me close my tower on my first day of work, welcomed us in and launched into a story. "In 1967, there were only nine lifeguards," he told us. Nick was also a chiropractor who adjusted horses.

And the house next door, 104, made for a convenient setup, two homes with open-door welcome mats. I walked in and found lifeguards making food in the kitchen and hosing off in the backyard. Out front were at least five VW vans of all colors parked on the street. I could hear guitar music playing, and towels hung over the side mirrors to dry. Fred Forsch, one of my fellow rookies, crawled under his van with a foil pan, deciding it was a good place to change his oil.

The homes were across the freeway, about two minutes from the state park. Kim and I stood together and watched as more people showed up. Beer runs to Tony's Market brought in cases of Coors. It became a party.

Decades later, I asked Nick what it was like to share his space with so many people. The pragmatic side of me wondered who cleaned the toilets and scrubbed the kitchen. Nick wrote back, "It seemed natural. Our door was open. A big party was just everyone over at once."

By my second summer at Pendleton, there were four of us—lifeguards of the female persuasion. We were called the gals, girls, chicks, and sometimes by our names. The men fell hard for Kim. She got a nickname within a week: "Kimmie." Big Schmo set up camp in our living room. He was tall, loud, and sucked the air out of a room. I wanted him off my sofa and out of Kim's life.

I didn't get a nickname. I was the kind of woman men had to get to know first.

The other part of our foursome, Erin and Sandy, were new to Pendleton, but not to lifeguarding.

Erin and I had been close since Saddleback. She showed up with surfboards, Huntington experience, and quiet strength.

Sandy Groos was a San Clemente local, with a lifetime of ocean credentials. She'd transferred from the City Lifeguards, looking for a better match. Pendleton, she hoped, was that place.

Together, the four of us wrote our chapter for the revised version of *The Feminine Mystique*.

Four women with different builds, backgrounds, and styles. No pigeonhole could contain us. We didn't have any trial period for test friendships. We became each other's sisters and bonded fast.

All guards, no matter their self-proclaimed tribe, faced the biggest test every summer—the Fourth of July. For lifeguards, the Fourth wasn't a celebration of freedom but a day to survive. No one dared call it "just another day." That kind of talk invited a karmic tsunami—mayhem with a side of the unimaginable.

On the Fourth, California beaches turned into battlefields. After a couple of summers working the holiday, I came to work hoping the day would end before it started. Visitors reverted to lawlessness, lost all reason, and let patriotism fuel an anything-goes free-for-all. The louder, the drunker, the better.

"Don't worry, he's friendly," a woman said as she shoved her pug at a little kid making a sandcastle near the water's edge. But on the Fourth of July, the child went to pet Pookie on the head, and the tiny, smushed-faced dog that had never hurt a flea, turned and bit the child's hand.

Beer bottles became weapons to break on each other's heads during family gatherings, while granny, sitting next to her walker, watched her progeny. With her face red from a sunburn and anger, she shook her finger in the air and yelled, "OK y'all, it's time to stop messin' around. Let's eat."

And people who had never entered the ocean, much less surfed, thought this would be a good day to go in the water fully clothed and catch a wave like they'd watched on *Hawaii Five-O.*

By the time my 11-hour Doheny shift ended, I was spent. The "holiday" had come and gone in a blur of bodies, noise, and nonstop action.

The campground shower line was long, but I waited for a cold-water rinse to wash away my distaste for the celebration. Once home, I put Creedence Clearwater's "Bad Moon Rising" on the record player. But noise, any noise, bugged me, and I jerked the needle off the album. I crawled deep into my bed and created a cocoon to shelter my ears from the war-zone noise of bottle rockets and sirens around me.

Eventually, like all days, the earth turned, and the Fourth ended. I woke up to July 5th—just another date. But not for the lifeguards of Pendleton.

Mike, the man with the big biceps, frowned at me and placed me at Doheny for a second day. The beach still smoldered from the night before, and sand was sparse, visible only between piles of trash. It was not a good day to go barefoot. Crowds were hungover from whatever poison they'd picked, and I staggered out to my tower with an extra-large lunch to make my day more tolerable.

From my tower, the morning started quietly. Smells from bonfires and ash mixed with the salty, moist air, and I imagined a toxic stew landing on my skin.

Scanning the beach, I let my thoughts drift to the men I worked with. In packs, they swaggered—competitive, loud, posturing masculinity.

But one-on-one with me, without the man-on-man bravado, these boys cracked wide open, confessing relationship dramas, doubts about their place in the pecking order, and questions they'd never ask one another.

"What do women really, truly want?"

"What about facial hair?"

"How many dates before sex?"

"Help me with my girlfriend."

Alone with a creature of the opposite sex, they seemed to think I held the secret answers for every woman in the world. I loved it. I had a front-row seat to the unfiltered lives of men—the good, the bad, and the ugly. I wish I'd taken notes.

And when things got too vulnerable, there'd be a crack in their voice, a pause without words, and they'd fart, make animal noises, and tell sex jokes.

The beach remained quiet and the water still. But I smelled something off. I tilted my head to the sky and took a big breath through my nose. The odor was warm, like the sweet and spicy tea I loved. The smell shifted to something sour, and I checked inside the tower for an old piece of rotted fruit or something growing moldy in a hidden corner.

Another smell joined the brew, pungent and gamy, and I scanned the beach for a dead sea lion. Nothing was in view, so I lifted my arms to check my T-shirt, which I hadn't washed in a few days. What was this smell?

The beach remained quiet, and I obsessed over the puzzle.

The unit made its first morning patrol and drove slowly toward me, Tower 6, the southernmost post guarding the water at Doheny.

I squinted at the approaching unit and blinked. From a distance, it looked like the Flintmobile. It wobbled and swayed in the sand, and I half-expected to see bare feet powering stone wheels through the Bedrock dust. Were Fred Flintstone and Barney Rubble driving?

My imagination ran wild, but finding real cavemen at Pendleton wasn't hard.

Franklin drove with his signature shock of hair so blond it turned white. And while his hair was bright, his intellect wasn't. Marcel sat shotgun—tall, lanky, and always with something fun, sexy, and sideways to say.

When they parked at the base of my tower, the smell intensified, and my eyes started to water.

"Are you going to the party tonight?" Franklin asked.

Marcel gave me a big grin, "Of course she is."

They stared at me, and heat rose through my neck and face. Suddenly, the smell thickened into a fog—sparkling, charged—encircling all three of us. We sat in a bubble of pheromones, the possibility of sex, the oozing, ever-present tension of working with men at the top of their physical game. And I was at the top of mine, with different body parts.

Of course I was going to the party. I had my pirate costume all planned out. Kim and I were meeting after work to eat and then heading over to 106 Santa Inez for the party of the year, the celebration marking the end of the Fourth of July.

Santa Inez was Ground Zero for the Fifth of July party. Five kegs were on ice, and the band made its last sound checks. Lifeguards in costumes, and San Clemente locals in the know about the Fifth of July party, made the holy pilgrimage to the party.

Kim and I waited in front for Sandy and Erin to make our grand entrance. "Hear ye, hear ye, the women of Pendleton have arrived." We entered the backyard arm in arm, and no one noticed. The party was well underway and jam-packed with people.

We dropped our foursome act and split up to check out the scene. I went toward the kegs, found a red plastic cup, and got in line for a beer. Ken's shark costume was fantastic, and underneath the get-up, he was one of the hunkiest guys I'd ever met. Lori, his longtime girlfriend, was dressed as Wonder Woman. She was tight on his arm, and the best I could manage was, "Great costume, Ken."

My eye patch and T-shirt were weak, but my arms looked strong, so I gave myself a few points for effort. Kim wore a black-satin Playboy bunny onesie with a puffed tail and cute ears. Men begged for her attention.

Boner stood in the middle of the crowd dressed as a rooster, the undisputed cock of the night. A towering, feathered headdress, right out of a Vegas show, crowned his head. Ray-Bans, and a tight, tiny, striped tank top stretched across his chest. And the main show—two torpedo-shaped silver-and-red projectiles that covered his own smaller cargo.

He was a perfect trifecta of ego, beauty, and swagger.

Slightly elevated, shoved up against the backyard fence, the band made its last sound checks. Duct tape covered electric cords that ran to open sockets throughout the house. Longman, my boss, his hair slicked back '50s style, played the keyboard. Eddie V. played the guitar and shaved his head for the shock factor. Scott came as he was, sans make-believe, and played the bass guitar. Tim played guitar in a World War II army uniform and looked gorgeous as usual. A guy I didn't know, a guard from years past, played the drums.

And then came the opening, *Green Onions*, the song we craved. It was the taste of chips, salsa, and that first sip of a margarita—a hint at pleasures to come. Longboard and the Knotty Knees, Pendleton's homegrown band, launched in epic and expected fashion. *American Graffiti* made this Booker T. & the M.G.'s track iconic, but we knew the truth: *our* band, the Knotty Knees, did it a zillion times better. We owned that song. My skin prickled with goosebumps. Without any hallucinogens, I became one with the world. The music wrapped me in a warm blanket of belonging until the Fifth of July surged through me and it was time to dance.

It took less than ten notes for the crowd to explode. Beers dropped, people screamed and ran close to the stage. This was Nick's backyard, a neighborhood in the small community of San Clemente, and it now held over 100 people. The lawn was a churned-up mess of mud, trampled grass, and beer.

The Knotty Knees didn't take a break. *Wipe Out* was a cult favorite, and we danced with religious fervor. As the song wound down, I took my pirate shirt to my forehead to wipe the sweat off my face, topped off my beer, dropped it, and ran back for more Clapton, Doors, Outlaws, and Hendrix. All familiar, yet better because my band played it.

The dancing blurred into hours of sweat, beer, and music. Little clouds of pot drifted from less crowded corners of the yard. The kegs ran dry, and the responsible guards went and bought more.

Before the party, Kim and I had discussed who might garner our attention. The beat changed, and the music slowed as Clapton's *You Look Wonderful Tonight* put a coupling mode in play. I looked around, a little lost and lonely, and was pulled into a foursome, rocked back and forth with Kim, Sandy, and Erin.

Sandy whispered the plan first: "Naked pier jump." The details spread by osmosis, and 10 of us ended up hiding our clothes at the base of the San Clemente Pier. We ran naked on the splintered planks. I ran behind Fast Freddy and laughed at his little frog butt, his legs spinning like he was pedaling a tricycle. At the end of the pier, we looked at the dark water below, then at each other, and jumped. We were drunk enough to think this was the best life had to offer, and sober enough not to drown.

That night, the police left us alone. We'd been chased before by the city cops: "Attention in the water, come directly to shore." But they were fools and never figured out how to catch us or find our clothes.

The water gave me a jolt, a cleansing of the mud and beer, and also told me I'd had enough. I put my clothes back on, feeling a little more modest than the initial strip down. It was time to call it a night. I was tired, saltwater-cleansed, and needed to sleep. Tomorrow would be July 6, and there was a lot of summer left.

After my third summer lifeguarding, on May 24, 1981, I planned to walk into the Aztec Bowl, shake a few hands, and collect my diploma from San Diego State University. But when dispatch called with an available shift, I didn't hesitate. I said yes.

John—I didn't feel comfortable calling him "Mulva"—was my partner for the day.

"Hey, hey, hey. It looks like we're working together." John smiled. We'd come a long way since his first hands-on-hips declaration. "We'll see if you can cut it."

We were the 8 a.m. first unit on duty, 4501, heading south past the old Nixon Estate, Cotton's Point, and the Trestles surf breaks. At Lowers, we pulled over to check on a surfer holding his foot.

"Shit," the young man sat next to his surfboard, clenching his jaw. "I don't think I've ever felt this kind of pain."

I glanced at his heel and saw the telltale stingray sting. We called it a "hit," a small puncture wound with a minor laceration, just enough to unleash the venom.

Stingrays, sleek, flat, and diamond-shaped, hid just beneath the sand in shallow, warm water until a foot stepped on their bodies. The attack wasn't personal; it was the stingray's Darwinian survival thing.

The surfer sat, rocked back and forth, knees tight to his chest, teary-eyed, and pleaded, "Make it stop. Please make it stop." I think he wanted his mom, and I was the closest thing to her in that moment.

"I heard peeing on it helps?" he asked, desperate for anything.

John grabbed a hot pack from the back of the unit, squeezed the bag, and shook it to activate the heat. The only real treatment to lessen the pain was soaking the foot in water just shy of scalding, hot enough to break down the venom. Regardless, we didn't have either.

"Hang in there," I told him. "Find hot water. Watch for infection." That was the best we could do.

His friend offered him a ride home. There was no lifeguard headquarters at Trestles yet. Just sand, pain, and the search for hot water.

"Poor guy," I said to John. "My friend Leslie got hit three times in a row down in Carlsbad. She said it felt like hot knives in her foot, and a few days later, she ended up in the ER with an infection." I shuddered just saying the words.

John went quiet, an unusual state for him. I stopped talking and gave him space.

We drove south to the Trails, beyond the San Onofre nuclear power plant—four miles of mostly deserted beach, leased to the State Parks from the Camp Pendleton Marine Base.

I remembered my first time working the Trails as a rookie. It was a solitary venture. At Trail 4, the midpoint of the park, I used my 2316 key to open the maintenance closet, tucked inside a concrete bathroom structure. Next to a broom, a hose, toilet paper, and cleaning supplies were my tools. I clipped the rescue tube around my waist, grabbed my first-aid kit and fins with one arm, and wrestled a folding webbed chair with the other. On my back was a canvas bag stuffed with my towel, jacket, lunch, and binos. I looked like a pregnant pack mule, heavily burdened and slow.

I walked along the flat plateau for five minutes with no sand or surf in sight, just the ocean horizon. The low scrub, the smell of sage, and the pungent blend of chaparral made me think of rattlesnakes as I stepped through their perfect habitat.

At the end of the bluff, like San Clemente, the trail dropped through sandstone walls and opened onto the Trail 4 beach.

I set up my beach chair like I was ready for a picnic, organized my tube and equipment, and used my binoculars to scan for signs of life. There was no one else on the beach.

Eventually the unit pulled up.

"You got enough water? It's gonna be a scorcher," Larry said, handing me a portable radio. He grinned. "And do you know about the naked people at Trail 6?"

I laughed, but I didn't know about the naked people.

"We'll be back after we deliver radios and give you a good break." They drove off, and I watched until the unit became so small it disappeared.

Summers later, back on the early morning unit shift with John, I took a deep look at him—intelligent, kind, and a basket of contrary ideas. I expected to hear his laugh come out of nowhere—his booming, ever-present laugh usually heard before he was seen.

Years later, he wrote to me about working with the four women of Pendleton: "When I became a lifeguard, I was an outsider. I was an Inland Tanker, an Okie from Bakersfield. I remember what it felt like to be judged. On the first day we worked together, you made a spectacular rescue, and any doubt or apprehension dissipated like Tule fog, instantly vaporizing into the ether. I felt the same way about Kim, Erin, and Sandy. Not only did you women do the job, you excelled."

He wanted me judged fairly. Yet he still wanted to be the judge.

In the unit, John talked with me about how to move forward in the lifeguard ranks. He encouraged me to get my Emergency Medical Technician certification and gave detailed advice on navigating the State Parks bureaucracy and the promotion process to become a full-time lifeguard.

"Make sure you don't miss the deadline to apply. We need to get you in the top three ranks. You can do this."

Once the business of my future was covered, we gossiped about other guards and traded recipes. Some days turned personal—our lives beyond the beach, love, and relationships. John was a sensitive man, quick to share kindness, even tears. I loved my days working with him.

That summer, I became a seasonal supervisor, or as it was called at Pendleton, a "seasonal stupidvisor." Regardless of the title, it was a huge vote of confidence. To earn the respect of my mentors, I was given an extra 29 cents an hour—not to boss guards around, but to model myself as a worthy guard. Pendleton had a code of humility, and if I put myself on a pedestal, there were plenty of guards to knock me off.

By that fall, big changes came fast. I was working dispatch in the little white tower above San Clemente, the same tower where I had parked on my first day of work years earlier, and I heard honking, a siren, and a circus-like tune over a microphone. I looked behind HQ, and a little parade of guards made their way to me, arms open, bringing hugs, flowers, and a bottle of champagne.

The hiring list was out, and I was offered a permanent lifeguard position at Huntington State Beach. If I accepted, I would become the first woman lifeguard in all of California to be promoted to a full-time ocean lifeguard.

I heard Nick's voice in my head from Easter Sunday, four summers earlier, just out of rookie school, working Tower 1: "What does it feel like to be the first woman?" Once again, I didn't know. Not yet.

I said yes. Lifeguarding had become my life.

Sally Tuttle, Pt. Mugu Rescue, 1975

Kiane Nowell, Los Angeles City, 1973

Wendy Paskin, the Saddleback Carry, 1974

Huntington Beach Lifeguards, 1966

1979 Pendleton Coast
Erin Porter, Kim Raymont, Sandy Groos, Debbie Friedman

Ingrid Loos, Bruce Baird, dory racing, 1982

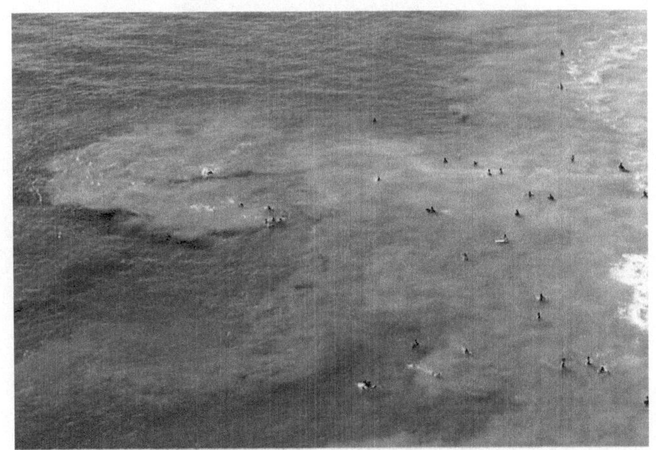

Rip Current, Huntington Beach

Debbie Friedman, John Topar, Bill Kramer,
Huntington State Beach, 1983

Patty and Kathy Richards, South Carlsbad Junior Lifeguards, 1974

Kim Raymont, Sandy Groos, Debbie Friedman,
San Clemente State Beach, August 1985

Joyce Hoffman, City of Del Mar Lifeguards, 1971

Calla Allison, Bodysurfing, Ventura, 2023

8

## *A Tale of Two Guards*

The Strand Boys loved Karlyn.

Hired as a State Park lifeguard in 1982 to work the Silver Strand, Karlyn Pipes brought everything the Strand Boys wanted in a woman lifeguard. She was loud, wild, and dove into their world without fear.

Karlyn was a high-level competitive swimmer and already had two years of guarding under her belt. She'd worked as a lifeguard for the Naval Air Station in Coronado, and when south swells came in, she'd made rescues in eight-to-ten-foot surf.

Karlyn decided to try out for a State Park lifeguard job. She finished in the top pack of the competitive swim, completed training, and earned her spot at the Strand. Her boyfriend, Raapman, was already part of the crew, which gave her an instant "in" with the tight-knit squad.

133

I first met Karlyn in 1983 at the Muriwai Surf Club on New Zealand's North Island. California lifeguards bumped into each other at different surf clubs as we made our pilgrimages across the island for surf, fresh milk, and free bunks.

Before I called her decades later, my mind's eye saw a picture: Karlyn and I standing together, outside the surf club, grinning like old friends. Curious, I dug through a box labeled "NZ" and found the photo. It was just as I remembered.

When I called Karlyn after all these years, both of us now in our 60s, it was as if no time had passed. She laughed easily, unfiltered with her words, and offered a blunt assessment of her younger self.

"I partied, surfed, and could drink as much as any of the guys. I could also kick ass in the water," she said with pride. "It helped me become one of the guys."

"We worked hard and played hard," Karlyn wrote me. "Surf trips to Mexico, nights out in Tijuana and Rosarito, plenty of tequila shots, some of which may or may not have involved nudity."

Karlyn woke in the morning, surfed, opened her lifeguard tower, and kept her water safe. She locked up at the end of the day and joined her fellow guards to drink and party through the night shift. "My party-girl attributes went a long way. Not to mention I had a nice set of boobs."

On my desk sat the book Karlyn wrote and encouraged me to read: *The Do-Over: My Journey from the Depths of Addiction to World Champion Swimmer*. Karlyn's story was much bigger than her time as a lifeguard. I found her frank storytelling and her difficult path to sobriety inspiring.

But in 1977, six years before Karlyn joined the crew, Janet Wardell became the first woman lifeguard on the Silver Strand State Beaches. And Janet did not get the love. She wasn't trying to break barriers or make a statement. "I loved the ocean and needed a job," she told me. "The Silver Strand beaches were close enough to bike to work from my home in Chula Vista."

She arrived as a rookie lifeguard, bringing national-level swim credentials, a strong 5-foot-11 frame, and the top rookie finish among the four new guards working the Strand. Still, the Strand disregarded her qualifications and high marks in training as they prepared new hurdles for their first woman lifeguard.

After graduating from lifeguard training, before Janet could even put on her red suit, Bob Isenor, the man who ran the State Park lifeguard program, pulled her aside and said, "If you mess up, you blow it for all women."

I cringed as she shared the story, picturing Janet towering over Isenor—a short, stocky man, his uniform shirt pocket bulging with a pack of cigarettes—as he told her that the future of all women lifeguards rested on her shoulders.

What was he thinking? Was this supposed to be helpful? Did he want to scare her?

Women were already working as State Park lifeguards at Ventura, Huntington, and San Diego State beaches. Isenor knew this. Janet didn't.

A year later, my first year as a new guard, I escaped the "Isenor talk." He was revered for creating the State Park lifeguard program. But he was also feared. Senior lifeguards pulled me aside and warned me to watch for the pale-green sedan with the State Park emblem on the door.

"He could pull up at any moment," they said, "and if he doesn't like what he sees, you're fired."

With Isenor's parting words to Janet about the future, shoulders, and blowing things, she arrived as a rookie lifeguard at the Strand. The district stretched from Silver Strand State Beach near Coronado, past Imperial Beach, and down to Border Field State Beach, where the United States and Mexico met in the fluid boundaries of the Pacific Ocean. At low tide, people could walk from Border Field to Tijuana in either direction, crossing the border with ease.

On her first day at work, Janet opened the employee door, walked into the lifeguard headquarters as instructed—and found herself face-to-face with naked men in the showers.

The guards made no effort to shield her from their communal space, where they made dick jokes and bragged about imaginary conquests. Ralph was the loudest and most brazen, his belly shaking like Jell-O when he laughed.

It was an X-rated cartoon, a bad dream, a swirl of wet, naked bodies. They didn't look like the Hollywood version of lifeguards. To Janet, they looked small and weak compared to the strong, competitive swimmers she trained with.

She blinked, swallowed hard, and kept moving. "I was 18

and embarrassed," Janet said. "But I didn't turn around. I just kept walking. There was no other way to get to dispatch."

She stood tall and headed for the spiral stairs and hoped to find a useful lifeguard who would tell her where she was supposed to work on her first day. With her assignment in hand, she left. She had a tower to get to.

"Where exactly will women change their clothes and go to the bathroom?" was the enduring chant of men guards in those years when the topic of women lifeguards came up along the California coast.

In most agencies, locker-room doors read simply "Men" and women had to improvise, reminded that they were different.

But the Strand Boys flipped the script. Instead of privacy, they marked their territory with naked bodies—a public, unapologetic display of towel-snapping and manhood-measuring to make sure Janet knew she didn't belong.

As her first summer progressed, Janet continued to show up, on time, ready, and alone. She parked her bike next to her day's tower assignment and looked at the lone tower box in the sky, sitting on a concrete pedestal. The deck sat six feet off the ground with no ladder to climb up into the tower.

Janet scanned her water, circled to the blind side—the back of the tower—and tossed her jacket, towel, water bottle, and binoculars up onto the platform, just over her head. She took a deep breath, planted her hands, and pushed her weight into her arms, pressing them straight in a full muscle-up until her body cleared the edge. With a grunt, she hauled herself up and leaned forward again to check her water.

Decades later, Janet, now 67, remembered, "What bugged me most was climbing up the back of the tower and not being able to see my water."

It didn't end with the press-up into the tower.

"They didn't think I was fast enough or cool enough if I didn't leap off the deck on my way to make a rescue," Janet said.

The Strand cowboys with their "yahoo" moves weren't taking care of basic business. They tested Janet but didn't hold themselves to any real standard. They put visitors' and each other's lives at risk. They had gone rogue.


Lifeguards drove south on the Border Field beach to a patchy, rust-red corrugated-steel wall, about five to six feet tall, that jutted 40 yards into the ocean, marking the political divide between the U.S. and Mexico.

On Sundays, the lifeguards climbed out of their unit, looked through gaping holes in the wall beyond the border, behind the sandy Playas de Tijuana, and heard thunderous screams and clapping. The sand shook beneath their feet. They could feel and see the *Plaza Monumental*, the "Bullring by the Sea," in Tijuana.

The stadium held up to 20,000 people, locals and tourists, all crowded close together in the massive arena to watch the bull, the toreador, or both, die.

Once the blood was let, and the last "Ole!" was shouted, the arena emptied onto the *playa,* and thousands of people flocked into the water. Older Strand guards remembered running into another country, not needing a passport, to make rescues in Mexico.

Many years ago, I stood where Janet had once worked. I waded out into the water, stood beside the rusty wall, and put my big toe into Mexico. With the rest of my body grounded in the U.S.A., my toe sat in a different history, culture, food, languages, political systems, laws, and ideas about swimming in the ocean.

The absurdity of the wall, separating very different countries while the ocean ignored it, reminded me of the Strand Boys. Their boundaries were arbitrary, and at times cruel. They bounced off each other for approval, turning outsiders like Janet into easy targets.

In professional lifeguarding, walls don't work. You have to have each other's backs.

Shut your eyes and imagine: a bull escapes from the *Plaza Monumental,* runs around the rusted wall into Border Field, and gores you, an unlucky lifeguard standing next to the unit without a toreador cape.

And the guards who ran down the beach to save your sorry ass? They didn't think twice about helping you, even if you'd treated them like shit the day before.


For eight summers, Janet stayed and worked as a lifeguard on the Silver Strand. She did not become one of the Strand

Boys, nor did she try. Most of the guards she worked with didn't reach out to her to create friendships, and Janet didn't reach back.

"I was extremely shy and uncomfortable with my appearance," she said.

Janet shared something with me that most young guards felt but rarely spoke aloud. For guards fortunate enough to work at beaches with strong leadership, early fears often gave way to confidence and growth. But without support, lifeguarding can be an incredibly lonely experience.

For Janet, the mission to save lives was a calling, a passion, and a deeply personal experience. She jumped out of towers, made rescues, worked as a unit guard, and wanted to promote. But the pedestal was always raised, and she was ignored. She watched as younger men with fewer skills moved into supervisor roles, and she remained silent. On still, quiet mornings, with the ocean glassy and calm, she thought about a future as a lifeguard. But without support—someone to mentor her through the system—promotions were elusive.

My path was different. I didn't know Janet then, but by her third year on the Strand, I had already earned a promotion to seasonal supervisor at Pendleton. A year later, I became a career lifeguard. I wasn't a better lifeguard than Janet, but I had mentors, a clear path, and people who encouraged me to move forward.

"It wasn't about the men," she said. "I loved the ocean. I was not going to let anyone drown in my water."

One August day, Janet's third summer guarding, she saw the lifeguard unit heading toward her tower and knew break time was near. She nodded to the guards, grabbed her fins, and jumped off the tower with no ladder, angry that it felt like a stunt. But her mind shifted quickly to the surf. She didn't waste a second.

Janet ran out into the water, put her fins on, and looked back at her tower. She was free until the unit turned on its red flashing lights, the signal to return to the tower.

Janet stroked out into the surf she'd watched all morning. The first wave approached, and she waited. Another one offered temptation, ready to break, but she said *no* and dove deep under its face, feeling her entire body absorb the bubbles of energy as she popped out the back. And then, the wave she wanted and waited for. The biggest wave of the set was coming just for her, just to make her day.

Janet popped up like a sea lion for a quick read and considered the exact place for the best takeoff. She backstroked into position, and with the momentum of the cresting wave, facing shore, she stretched both arms forward. She became a torpedo without the intent to harm, only the peaceful desire to become part of a wave.

With a full-body dolphin kick, a powerful undulation, Janet disappeared for a brief moment as she merged underwater and into part of the wave's face. This was her favorite part of bodysurfing: no surfboard, no crowds fighting for position in the surf zone, no judges prepared to score tricks. For Janet and most bodysurfers, the simplicity created the magic.

In this brief moment, one she'd felt thousands of times before, she was in the wave. Her head and right arm popped out of the water first as she felt her legs lifted, flying horizontal to the base of the wave. She flew high speed across the unbroken face of the water, moving on the right shoulder, away from the peak. In the realm of bodysurfing, this was the ultimate freedom ride.

From shore, only her head and arms broke the surface. The rest of her body was a glazed silhouette, a crystallized shadow in the translucent wave. Her orange fins sparkled behind her, the last part of her body not yet eaten by the whitewater. It was easy to imagine she was a sea nymph, playing with dolphins.

Once the wave lost speed, Janet kicked out the back of the wave and smiled. The ocean felt like home, her place of peace and joy.

Before she swam out again, Janet looked to shore and saw the flashing lights. Break time was over. She caught a small wave and rode the whitewater to shore. Janet walked backward to the base of her tower and stood next to the unit. Ralph, the Jell-O-bellied naked man, said, "Nice wave."

Janet didn't answer. She turned slowly and looked at his balding head, and then through him with steely eyes.

He flinched first with a nervous giggle.

She climbed up the back of the tower, wrapped her towel around her waist, and scanned the water. The unit drove off, and she smiled. Janet was not going to let anyone drown in her water.

9

# *Crash Course Huntington*

In the fall of 1981, I was promoted to the Orange Coast District—Huntington and Bolsa Chica State Beaches—for my first permanent lifeguard assignment. By winter, I was in Pacific Grove for BPOT, Basic Peace Officer Training. I was one of 12 Lifeguards training alongside State Park Rangers.

California State Parks managed more than 250 units and 1.4 million acres, including over 300 miles of coastline—the longest protected stretch in the nation. That meant everything from the remote, empty, unguarded beaches of Humboldt County to packed urban beaches of Southern California, where tensions ran high, and drinking the most alcohol was considered a sporting event. The work could shift from calm to full-blown crisis in seconds. And local police backup wasn't always coming.

The training center was on the Asilomar Conference

Grounds, a century-old coastal retreat, designed by Julia Morgan, California's first licensed woman architect. To reach the ocean, I walked past weathered, redwood-sided buildings and stone chimneys, framed by Monterey pines. Within minutes, I saw the white sands and cold water of Asilomar State Beach. This coast was foreign to me, a SoCal girl. The smell of kelp and pine filled my lungs, so different from Huntington's smell of car exhaust and burning tires.

Back in class, beauty gave way to business. I was training to wear a badge and carry a gun. I knew it was part of the job I signed up for as a full-time lifeguard, but it didn't seem real yet. At Pendleton, the permanent lifeguards I'd worked with kept their guns in a lockbox in the center console of the unit. Working with Nick, a permanent, I wondered if the gun would fire every time we hit a pothole or dropped into a low spot in the sand. But I kept my questions to myself and pretended to know more than I did, especially after all the years I'd spent watching *Starsky & Hutch* shootouts on TV.

We weren't like Los Angeles County, San Diego City, or other lifeguard agencies. We were lifeguards with badges and guns, enforcing laws far beyond dogs off leash. But State Parks was the only system I knew.

We entered rooms with rubber mats, pretended to be "bad guys" and did make-believe tackles with batons and handcuffs. I wrestled my classmates to the ground and laughed nervously, still not believing I would arrest someone.

And there were guns with real bullets. My distaste for weapons didn't surpass my desire to be a full-time lifeguard. So, I sat in class and learned lessons about criminal law, the penal code, and firearms. At the firing range, I drew my revolver out of my holster, held my gun still, lined it up with the target, and hit the center most of the time. I could separate my dislike of law-enforcement work from the satisfaction of hitting a bullseye.

For lifeguards, sitting at a desk for hours was punishment. When the schedule called for physical training, we were the first ones out the door. On this day, it was a jog through the narrow streets around the training center, under the wind-bent cypress trees, past tiny front yards carpeted with pine needles.

On a break, relieved to be moving again, I ran with two classmates—Mike "Mestri" Silvestri and John Topar—new permanent lifeguards like me. We fell into an easy rhythm, right foot, left foot, breathing at the same pace, in and out, enjoying fresh air.

The noise hit me first. One second, we were jogging past a tiny house with gingerbread trim, and the next, I was in the air, my entire body and world now upside down. The first impact was a thud to my legs, breaking my right and crushing my left, and I watched in a slow-motion, high-speed, altered state as my body curled forward into a somersault.

The damage didn't stop there. The force of the collision, body versus car, sent my head into the windshield, dislocated my right shoulder, and somehow flipped me on top of the car's roof, sitting upright and backward.

Warm blood trickled down my face. Mestri and Topar climbed on the roof of the car and reached for me. I asked, "Is this what it feels like to die?"

There was no pain, only shock. I looked at both of them to help me understand what just happened. Sirens blared. People closed in around me, and two men eased me onto a stretcher. I floated above my body and watched as they loaded me into the ambulance.

When the doors swung open again, I saw the big red sign: EMERGENCY. There was a blur of activity around me as nurses called me "sweetie" and doctors asked for permission to operate on my left leg and close the wound on my forehead.

The days blurred, and I pressed a little button beside my bed when I needed water or wanted a wet cloth against my face and lips. The room smelled like bleach with a whiff of urine. There were no books or posters on the wall, just sterile white, and groans from my adjacent and hidden roommates. Movement hurt, and I chose to lie very still, trying not to trigger the pain. Kind nurses held my hand, and I didn't know what to ask or say. During the dark hours of the night, I cried as I tried to understand what was next. I wanted a plan and a path forward that took me back to the beach, but I couldn't see one yet.

Visitors trickled in and out: "Don't worry, Debbie, you'll get through this."

On the 10th day, my doctors decided that I would be flown back to Huntington Beach and start rehabilitation. My apartment was two blocks from the beach, close enough to hear the waves, but not strong enough to reach them.

With two leg casts, a sling for my right arm, and a big patch on the right side of my head, I was loaded on a gurney, put on a plane, and sent home with a walker, a calendar full of physical-therapy appointments, and my ignorant but unshakable belief that I'd be back on the beach by summer.

Bill Kramer was my new boss, in charge of Huntington and Bolsa Chica State Beach Lifeguards, overseeing 80 of us. He was also a bag full of mixed messages. He looked like he'd been the lifeguard supervisor at Huntington since the beginning of time. If the door to his office was ajar, I could peek in and see his feet on the empty wooden desk inside the white-stucco building with emerald-green trim, the same office where I'd interviewed for my seasonal lifeguard job years earlier.

But at night, he changed. With a beer in hand, his laugh was infectious. The aloofness disappeared, and he pulled his guards and friends in close. In those moments, he was all youth and vigor.

With my legs still in casts, my days filled with physical therapy and a restless drive to start my new career, I hobbled into Bill's office and proposed coming in to learn the administrative side of beach operations. I looked at him squarely, sad and determined, and said, "Bill, you know this makes sense. You pay me to work."

I didn't offer myself up for secretarial work. My strategy was to learn the guts of the lifeguard operation. Like all good guards from Pendleton Coast, the more I learned, the more I could say I knew. Washing a jeep meant that I had experience working in a unit. Once I announced my new skill, with a lie of omission about the driving part, I became eligible to drive a unit on the beach. This was one path to move up in the pecking order.

Bill shook his head and laughed, already turning away from me. He looked over his shoulder. "You're not joking?"

I laid out my plan. "Just pick me up in the morning at my apartment." I was still unable to drive, both legs in casts. "I promise, I'll be helpful." I'd already hit bottom, my body broken, so I begged. I had to do something besides imagine my future.

Bill grumbled, but in a comic twist, he drove to my apartment for over a month, watched me hobble down the stairs and climb into his tan State Park sedan, and drove us to work. We didn't exchange words, just his consistent nod of his head and a big sigh. He exited the vehicle, entered his office and shut the door. I followed behind, sat outside his room, and looked for things to read.

Bill didn't seem to have a problem with me as a new woman permanent lifeguard, but he didn't like me invading his space. He wanted to be left alone. I wanted his attention. Bill's management style was to leave well enough alone, and my eager-beaver, gung-ho, ask-a-million-questions attitude drove him nuts.

I never doubted my recovery; I just didn't understand that there would be a doctor with the final say, someone who could decide whether I was "fit enough" to return to duty. I got up every morning, did thousands of leg lifts, pumped iron, swam, and took every step I could until I ran back onto the beach.

The test that had once echoed around me—*Could Debbie, a woman permanent, cut it at Huntington, the so-called proving ground of State Park lifeguarding?*—had gone quiet. Most of the guards at Huntington State Beach didn't even know I existed.

In April, a few months after my accident, down to one cast and a sore shoulder that made sleep difficult, I saw signs that rookie training in the lifeguard garage was about to begin. I wanted to teach. And I needed to make it happen, immediately. I barged into Bill's office, my words harsher than I planned: "You know I'm right. I'm still on light duty."

He looked at me a little surprised and I backed off, tried to soften my attitude.

"Let me help with training. The new guards need to see a woman instructor."

My voice wavered. I cringed at the sound of myself.

Bill gave me a long, theatrical eye roll right into my face and put his hands on his hips. "Go over and talk to them," he said. "See if they'll have you."


I faced the rookie class, scanning thirty wet, messy, matted heads, and caught Mestri's grin at the back of the garage. He stood with Denny, another instructor from San Diego. They flashed two thumbs up each—a show of four—stuck out their tongues and pretended to bonk their heads together to make me laugh.

DP, my San Clemente friend and mentor, now working at Huntington, stood beside them with perfect posture, hands clasped on his belt. He smiled and nodded to let me know I was doing fine.

In the middle of the clammy room, thirty rookies slouched at attention. The place smelled like mildew and body odor. I flashed back to my seat in this room as a rookie. Now, five years later, I stood before the trainees, a cast on my lower right leg, and tried to look authoritative.

Beads of sweat formed on my forehead and under my arms. I wanted to blame it on the claustrophobic conditions in the room, but more likely it was the unspoken test I'd created in my mind. The rookies didn't know my story, and I didn't share it with them. I wanted them to see more than a woman in a cast. I needed to get out of my head and act like the lifeguard I was becoming.

Standing in front of the class with the other instructors, I was only a few years older than most of them. The rookies were on trial, and we were the judges and jury.

Whatever opinions these kids held about women lifeguards or women in general, they needed to think twice. Still, I scanned the room. What did they see when they looked at me? A cast. A woman. A broken body not yet ready to charge into the surf.

A quick breath, and I launched into the lecture.

"Shock," I told the class, "can lead to organ failure, even death, if you miss the signs. Pale skin, rapid pulse, shallow breathing…"

I paused and moved my gaze through the group. The room went still. I couldn't tell if I'd said something profound or if they'd slipped into REM.

In that stretch of silence, I saw Kelly Casey, one of two women, in the middle of the class. She gave me the smallest smile, and I smiled back.

*Mental note: Talk to her later. I want her story.*

After class, the rookies stacked the desks neatly, mopped the floors, and scrubbed the bathrooms. Kelly zipped her gear bag and limped out of the room. I followed her outside, stood beside her, and pointed at the ACE bandage wrapped around her left ankle.

"What's going on with your ankle?" I asked.

"I tripped on one of the runs a few days ago," she said. "The athletic trainer on my swim team's been taping it every night. That's OK, right?"

"Does it hurt?" I looked at the red, swollen toes sticking out from under her bandage.

She explained that she was driving to UCLA every night, over an hour each way, to have it taped.

"I know I can finish training."

We both went quiet.

Kelly finished in the top half of her rookie class.

By May, I was able to leap up to the high bar and peel off eight pull-ups. It was short of my personal best, but a decent show of strength. I kept swimming laps at Belmont Plaza, and for the first time in my life, I started running miles on concrete. Most important, I ran into the surf without hesitation, pulled on fins, swam between towers, and finished with a bodysurf session, catching waves without fear that my body might betray me. The doctors signed the official papers, and I was released to work as a lifeguard again.

My first summer at Huntington. I patrolled in my red swimsuit and white T-shirt, scanned the surf, and backed up tower guards on rescues. Meanwhile, my classmates who finished the Peace Officer Academy drove patrol sedans through the State Beach parking lots, working swing shifts into the night, arresting drunk drivers, and writing tickets for park violations. We'd trained together until my accident and now worked in separate worlds. I was grateful to work the beach, and remained in denial that I'd return to the Peace Officer training and eventually, carry a gun.

On the beach, I wasn't the only one starting fresh. Kelly and I were both rookies, but in different ways. She was a new seasonal lifeguard, working rookie schedules and learning how to guard Huntington and Bolsa Chica. I'd been promoted to beaches I'd never worked and needed the most basic experiences to understand the crowds, tricky currents, and mega rescues of my new home. Windy Bolsa Chica taught me to never, ever, forget my jacket.

Kelly and I became friends—running and swimming before work, listening to each other's stories, and always finding a good laugh. We were ready to jump into the after-work scene, too. We entered competitions, went to the parties, and showed up for the workouts. Years later, she told me I was her "hot-chick training instructor." That still makes me laugh.

My Huntington shift started at 11 a.m., and there was no sign of Burt, my shotgun. He was late for work, and I was frustrated that he thought this was acceptable. Burt had a reputation. He was a self-anointed Waterman and walked with a puffed-up chest. But so far, I didn't see a good lifeguard. I wanted a partner who came ready to work and would share his experience so I could learn. So far, he was zero for two.

"Waterman" is a huge tent of a word, giving people plenty of space to dream and aspire.

The idea of proclaiming yourself a "Waterman" was the antithesis of everything I'd learned as a young guard in the tradition of the Pendleton ideal. Humility was a virtue, along with modesty. If someone called you a waterman to your face, the proper response was to laugh, deny it, and change the subject.

I think I knew a Waterman at San Clemente. His middle name was Duke, and he walked gently on the sand, barely leaving a footprint behind. He heard the whispers as people tried to give him the title, and he just smiled and averted his eyes.

After work, he threw a fishing line, no pole or hook, into the water, and within minutes, a fish would leap into his hands, begging to be sacrificed for his sustenance. This man was a fierce competitor, yet I'd never seen him out of breath. After winning a race, he stayed at the finish line to shake hands and offer kind words to his competitors. He knew where the rescues were before anyone else, and with the most genteel of instructions, he helped all the lifeguards become their best. Did I mention he played music, too, lived in his van, and showed up to the parties with the perfect girlfriend?

I wanted to be a Waterman, but Watermen are a myth, and the myth remains men-only. Still, I wanted fish to worship me, and the best-looking guy to show up on my arm at the parties.

What I learned from these self-proclaimed braggarts, who tossed the title among themselves at Huntington yet had a hard time showing up to work on time or without reeking of alcohol, was that they were just a bunch of dogs fighting over the same bone, desperately wanting each other's approval.

I was confused and then saddened that a group of Huntington guards blasphemed my fantasy.


Burt strutted toward me, late. I'd already checked out the vehicle. "You need to be on time," I waited for his excuse.

He climbed into the unit with his legs hanging out the side and looked backward, away from the water.

I drove straight out to Tower 15 and looked south—an unbroken line of towers and guards stretching all the way to the Santa Ana River.

High tide kept me driving up on the berm. Burt finally pulled his feet inside the vehicle and turned his attention to the water. I didn't like riding in a unit with someone who clearly didn't want to work with me. But that was his problem.

I pulled up beside Tower 14, Kelly's tower, and climbed up. We leaned on the railing and looked out at the surf.

"I heard you had some action this morning."

She threw her arms in the air and shook her head.

"Oh my God, Debbie. It was insane."

My bleached-out eyebrows lifted, "Tell me more."

"I wasn't even on duty," she said. "I got here early for a workout, and this little kid came sprinting up the beach, in full panic mode, yelling, 'There's someone hurt! Someone's hurt!'"

She shook her head, still caught in the moment.

"I climbed up, unlocked the tower, grabbed my tube and first-aid kit, no uniform—and just ran with him."

She talked at hyperspeed, and I wanted to hear every detail. But first, I raised a finger, paused, and did a focused scan of the water. It was easy to get distracted talking to another guard. I glanced at the unit below and saw Burt with his feet on the dashboard, focused on a burrito, not the ocean.

I looked straight ahead, bent my knees and waved my hands to my chest, *tell me everything*. We both spoke the language of talking forward, engaged, but not with our eyes. We told our story to the sea and trusted we had each other's attention.

"I get down there and see this woman sitting on a towel with curlers in her hair, those pink, foamy wrap things all over her head. She's got two kids, and one of them is sobbing, just totally hysterical."

She paused. "I ask the kid what happened, but the woman looks up at me and says, 'It's not him. It's me.' Then she lifts the towel, and"—Kelly's jaw dropped—"there's an umbrella pole sticking out of her upper thigh. She was impaled."

"Jeez," I shook my head.

"I know. The top had snapped off while she was trying to jam it into the sand. Somehow, the pole just drove straight through her leg."

I covered my mouth and chin, my mind raced to imagine it—a woman sitting calmly with a pole through her thigh.

"There wasn't even any blood," Kelly said. "I kept thinking, why is there no blood? I don't remember what I said to her. I just told the kid, 'Run back to the tower. Pick up the phone. Say someone's hurt really bad."

She kept going with the details. "The unit showed up fast, and then the paramedics. They cut and shortened the pole on both sides of her leg and loaded her on a stretcher in a sitting position with her knees bent. I watched them carry her off the beach like she was a queen."

Kelly ran her hand down her leg, still processing what she'd seen a couple of hours ago.

"Unbelievable." I was at a loss for words. "Do you need to jump in the water before we take off?"

"No, but can you find out what happened to her?" she asked, her voice unsteady.

I was a rookie, too, but I knew enough to say, "We rarely find out. You did well, Kelly."

Back in the jeep, I told Burt to drive, and we continued our patrol south. I wanted to share the story with him, but he wasn't proving himself to be a listening kind of guy.

Work was over for the day, and Kelly and I made plans to meet up after dinner at Tower 12, Newland Street. I parked my car and Kelly waved, waiting for me.

It was dusk, and there was a group of guards about 100 yards away, in the parking lot. "Let's go over and see what's going on tonight," I grabbed Kelly by the sleeve.

We walked closer, then stopped. Something was off, a gut feeling, and I put my arm out to stop her. We stayed just on the edge, spectators now.

"Let's hang here."

I looked at the men, many of whom I'd worked with a few hours earlier, and they were barely recognizable. Their faces were red and splotchy. Beer dripped down their bulging necks, mixed with sweat and sand. I was repulsed.

A few of them stood in a tight cluster, pushed their chests out, fists clenched in an attempt to walk in a perpetual flex. *Were they trying to attract someone? Each other?* There was no Schwarzenegger strength here. It looked like they were straining on a communal toilet.

Beer cans were passed around and sprayed like fire hoses. Foam flew out of mouths, and cans smashed on foreheads. Shirts came off. Primal grunts followed. They slammed into each other, pounding their chests and thrusting their hips like animals performing mating rituals.

It was grotesque. It was loud. It was ridiculous, but not funny.

They didn't know Kelly and I were watching. This ritual wasn't for us; it was for themselves. A performance of testosterone gone wild, the "Big T." There was no self-awareness, but they were fully locked in. Something deeper than thought: dominance, instinct, maybe even fear, had taken over.

Then it got louder. Wild-eyed and flailing, the group reached a fevered pitch. From the center of the hysteria, the chant began:

"R – O!"

"R – O!"

"R – O – C – O!"

"Rock Out! Rock Out! Rock Out with Your Cock Out!"

The men, now at the peak of ecstasy, threw their heads back and howled to the sky, offering thanks to their ROCO god. They dropped to their knees and thumped their chests—slow and hard, lost in raw, climactic glee.

Kelly and I stepped back. I gave an awkward laugh and shrugged, then felt ashamed. These were men we worked with, and I didn't want her to think this was normal.

*What do I say to Kelly?* I had no words.

I stayed close to her, feeling protective, and tried to make sense of what we were seeing. The party kept going, but the zenith had passed. The core group fell apart. Some wandered off to pee in the sand. One of the guards I'd worked with that day leaned over the divider wall between the parking lot and the beach and threw up. The scene ended with a whimper, and each man stumbled to dig a hole to crawl into. It didn't look like chasing women would be on the night's agenda.

I scanned the crowd for DP and the other mentors I trusted most. They weren't there. But I wasn't sure I wanted to talk to them about what I'd just seen.

ROCO wasn't new. It had existed for years before I arrived

and continued for decades after I left. In 2022, 60-year-old men showed up at lifeguard competitions with "ROCO" scrawled across their sagging chests in grease pencil. I wondered if they bragged to their grandkids at Thanksgiving: *I was a ROCO guard when I was your age.*

Many of these same men called themselves Watermen. The drunker they got, the bigger the rescue. The louder they yelled, the more legendary they became. Like the Waterman myth, ROCO didn't include women, and I never met a woman who wanted any part of them. To be part of the ROCO club, you just needed to be a dick.

I couldn't unsee what I'd seen. The man sitting next to me in the unit might've been a decent lifeguard, but I'd seen his ROCO side—reckless, mean-spirited, and cruel. After that, I couldn't fully trust him.

And it wasn't just beer and chanting. It went further.

ROCO boys lived for Angels baseball games, and more important, the buses that took them there. They squeezed themselves into seats packed with alcohol and started taking off their clothes, mooning cars along the I-5, and doing penis tricks for each other. Rookie hazing was ritualized, an initiation into the ROCO world. Senior guards filled their butts with water, held rookies down, and expelled it on them. One guard blacked out and woke up with his genitals painted green. That story became a legendary piece of ROCO lore.

There *were* lifeguards I trusted—men who stood apart. But there was nowhere for me to take my unease. No rule in the handbook said: This doesn't belong in lifeguarding, on or off duty.

When I was a lifeguard at Pendleton, full of drama in our own ways, I never witnessed cruelty. I romanticized the job. We were driven by purpose, integrity, and public service. But at Huntington, I met men who lifeguarded by day and chest-thumped by night. My illusion fractured.

Lifeguarding was built on trust, and I didn't trust these men. Not in the water. Not with rookies. Not beside me.

ROCO wasn't the entire culture at Huntington or Bolsa Chica. But it kept us from becoming the best lifeguards we could be. It excluded people and built violent myths instead of trust. It leaked into everything—our judgment, teamwork, and sense of safety.

At Pendleton, I'd grown up in a culture where lifeguards watched out for one another. Mistakes were corrected without humiliation. Competition pushed us to be better, not to break each other down. Huntington carried a sharp, unforgiving edge, and I never felt like every guard had my back.

Some still laugh about it. Others pretend it wasn't that bad.

I witnessed it. I remember. And I won't forget.

# 10

# *The Monster Rip*

It was August 1983, and inland temperatures were punishing. Weather stations warned that Riverside would hit triple digits, sending tens of thousands of people on an exodus west to the beach in search of relief.

Marcus was my scheduled partner at Huntington for the day. We made sure the unit was ready for patrol. I popped the hood, pulled the oil dipstick, wiped it clean, and got a good read. The radiator was topped off, I let the hood drop, and it slammed shut.

My hands reeked of oil, and even after a rinse, the smell stuck. I'd need a saltwater sand scrub to cleanse myself.

Marcus checked the tire pressure—full, but low enough for driving in the sand. The O2 tanks and first-aid kit: "Check." We packed extra water for the towers, threw on hats, and gave each other a nod.

I was superstitious and had nightmares about trying to make rescues without fins. Like touching a good-luck charm, I started every unit shift with a silent check. *Fins? Yes.*

I climbed the stairs in the new and improved lifeguard headquarters and found the dispatcher, Peter, deep in prep for the day. Two clipboards sat on his desk, one labeled "Lost Kids" and the other "Found Kids." In between was the schedule.

Peter looked at me, gave me a double thumbs up, and said, "It's all hands on deck today. Everyone is on duty, and I can smell rescues in the air."

From the third-story dispatch vista, the eyes in the sky, I scanned the beach. To my left, one mile south, was the Santa Ana River. A mile to my right, Tower 15, the northern border of Huntington State Beach. Fifteen brown lifeguard towers lined the two-mile stretch of beach, each marked with an orange placard and bold black numbers visible from a distance.

Beyond Tower 15, city lifeguard towers dotted the beach for another mile, all the way to the Huntington Pier.

Guards didn't want to cross the arbitrary line in the water between their city and state beaches. If a rescue or current pushed a guard over the imaginary line, guards sprinted back to safe sand. A move into each other's territory was like crossing into another country without a passport—a place with its own culture, values, uniforms, towers, rescue boats, and vehicles.

The state guards thought the city guards were uptight and a bunch of military wannabes, and the city guards thought we were out of control, macho, sloppy, and childish.

The boundaries had been peed on, and what was left was an uneasy détente, an unspoken agreement to leave each other alone.

Back at Huntington, it was a trek for beachgoers through a long stretch of sand to get to the water from the parking lot. From headquarters, it looked like colonies of ants moving toward something tasty to eat as visitors dragged their coolers, towels, and beach chairs into position for a day of fun, damn it.

The calls started coming over the radio immediately: "Unit 42, respond to Tower 8, two-person rescue."

The day became warm, and surf grew larger. The south swell created waves from 8 to 10 feet. The set waves grew bigger. I felt the sand—and then my body—vibrate with the swell's energy.

The tide shifted from high to an outgoing low, and rip currents began to pull hard, creating rivers of frothy, sandy, fast-moving water that pulled unsuspecting swimmers into the surf zone. And beyond.

We drove from one rescue to another, backing guards up, giving rides back to towers, and swimming out to make rescues when there were multiple victims.

This was Huntington at its best. All the egos and bullshit were left away from the beach. The guards worked together as a finely tuned machine. *Surfwatch,* the Huntington rescue boat, patrolled outside the surf and raced up and down the coast, backing up lifeguards and pulling victims on board. Relief guards didn't jog; they sprinted from tower to tower, and tower guards stood tall with hands on tubes, wanting to make another rescue.

Marcus and I responded to one call after another. Then came the radio call: "Unit 42, multiple victim rescue at Towers 12 and 13. Respond Code 3."

"Which tower did he mean, 12 or 13?" I questioned my shotgun. With lights and sirens, we drove north to Newland Street, Tower 12. We watched water spray off the bow of the bright-yellow Huntington *Surfwatch* as Captain Mel Tubbs paralleled our path in the water. Then the Bolsa *Surfwatch* rounded the Huntington pier at high speed from the other direction with Captain Rick at the helm.

*This is going to be big.* I felt my pulse quicken and gripped the steering wheel of the unit tighter.

A few minutes later, we were on the berm between Towers 12 and 13 and stood on the unit's seats with binoculars to better assess the situation. I saw lots of heads bobbing in the water and only a few rescue tubes.

Marcus and I locked eyes, stunned. To our left, and extending to Beach Blvd. at least five towers wide, we saw one humongous rip current. The rip wasn't just pulling between towers; it *encompassed* them. A raging river of salt water, a once-in-my-life rip, had formed, sucking everyone within its reach out to sea—a people-eating monster that pulled anything and everyone in its path in the wrong direction, away from shore.

Outside the waves, both *Surfwatch* vessels backed

their sterns slowly toward shore, into the head of the rip. Deckhands threw tubes and inflatable cushions to victims and started pulling people onto the boats. The captains of both vessels maneuvered carefully, keeping the twin-engine boats steady for boarding victims and spotting unseen rescues. Beneath the stern, propellers spun, a lethal danger for anyone too close.

Both captains held the bows steady, pointed seaward, while the sterns faced the maelstrom.

I called dispatch and said, "Unit 42, both guards out." Marcus and I sprinted to the water. Looking back, another lifeguard unit arrived, and more guards entered the water behind us, high-stepping, fins in hand, tubes released and flying high in the air as more guards charged into the rip.

Marcus and I swam next to each other. From deep within, I found an extra level of speed, pulling, kicking, and grunting. We slowed and started to look for victims. From Captain Mel's boat, a deckhand pointed at victims. I began passing my tube to swimmers. With a glance, I saw Kelly, out in the water before me, holding two victims on her tube. Another guard pushed victims onto the boat, while the deckhand pulled them to safety.

I grabbed two young boys holding a Styrofoam drugstore copy of a boogie board and swam them to *Surfwatch*. Tubbs waved me off and pointed to the Bolsa boat. He had three guards on board; it looked like 10 victims, and he needed to make room for more. He cleared the area and drove upcoast, clear of the rip, to find a safe spot to drop the victims and the lifeguards, who would swim them to shore.

Captain Rick and the Bolsa boat quickly filled with victims. Six guards, including me, continued to swim through the head of the rip, clipping in victims. The deckhand scanned the water from above and pointed at more. I made a secret deal with the god I did not worship. *Please let them all be found.*

More guards worked the inside surf and pulled victims to shore.

After 40 minutes of chaos and nonstop rescues, the Bolsa boat deckhand raised a fist to his head—Code 4. All clear. Everyone was safe.

I heard a unit's radio on shore blare out its announcement, "Stay out of the water. Move away from the water."

Captain Tubbs, steady as always, returned just in case there were more victims.

The white Huntington City rescue boat sat outside, ready to help. And the red city-lifeguard units sat on their side of the line in the sand, both guards standing on their seats, binos raised, as state guards were pushed into their territory by the south current.

Captain Rick steadied the Bolsa boat and signaled me and two other guards to swim to the boat, our last victims already on board. With his thumb up, the required signal to board, I climbed on the stepladder, through the transom, and sat on the deck. With my tube in hand and fins still attached to my feet, I steadied myself, looked back at the water with disbelief at the number of victims and lifeguards who just managed a killer rip spanning five lifeguard towers.

Kelly sat next to me on the boat deck. We watched over our victims as they huddled together, breathing hard, shaking, and silent, trying to make sense of what just happened to them. Grateful for the rescue boats, we sat on the sticky, non-slip deck and grinned at each other, a mix of excitement and fear about what had just taken place.

One dazed victim looked up and asked, "I was just getting my legs wet. Why am I on a boat?"

"Can you believe this?" Kelly whispered.

Then I saw a stranger holding a rescue tube. He was a city guard—thin, shivering, his head down. He looked like a prisoner of war, waiting to rattle off his name, rank, and serial number.

Rick took us into city territory so we would not drift back with the current into the rip. In between sets, he backed in slowly toward shore. I stood on the transom, holding my tube and wearing my fins, and watched Rick point, my signal to jump back into the water. Next in were the victims, ready for us to pull them safely to shore. The disembarking process went slowly until the victims were each paired with a guard and swam to the dry sand.

The city guard left without any parting words, looking desperate to go home. Back on the beach, we ensured that no one was in shock or had aspirated water. The mom of the Styrofoam boys ran down the berm as she saw me with her children. She hugged them tight and mouthed silently to me, "Thank you."

Guards returned to their towers, relief guards gathered at the units, and the Bolsa boat stayed at Huntington for a while as extra backup in case the monster rip was not an anomaly. Captain Tubbs left the scene heading south. On shore, the rest of us dried off and moved toward our assigned zones for rescues that would now seem small compared with what we had just experienced.

In that one rip current, over 40 people were rescued. There would have been more if the guards hadn't kept people out of the water. Most important, no one drowned. The response included five units, two *Surfwatch* boats, six tower guards, two relief guards, the HB City boat and unit that stood by, and a lone city guard who did the right thing.

Twenty-three guards saved forty-six lives, and prevented countless others from drowning that day. It was a good day to visit a well-guarded beach.

11

## *Bad Guys*

When I left for my permanent lifeguard position at Huntington Beach, it was clear: I'd carry a gun, fully trained and empowered under Section 830.2 of the California Penal Code—the same legal authority as California Highway Patrol, sheriffs, and city police agencies.

Between being hit by the car in 1981 and the cancellation of the academy the following year, I worked as a lifeguard on the beaches of Huntington for two years without a badge or a gun. Those years were a reprieve—no enforcement shifts—but it didn't last. From my cozy unit looking out to sea, a notification arrived that the academy was a go, and a seat had my name on it.

State Park Peace Officer Training was comprehensive, yet focused on academics and physically gentle compared with most police academies of the 1970s and 1980s. I graduated with the idea that cooler minds and common sense would prevail in most situations, and I'd figure out a way to live with my new gun-toting persona.

I returned to Huntington with a silver badge on my white uniform shirt, a state-issued gun belt heavy with gear—a Smith & Wesson revolver, a speed loader filled with bullets, handcuffs, and a canister of Mace. When I arrived at work, a baton sat beside a bowling bag holding my gear. No matter how deep I tucked the bulletproof vest into my shorts, it rode up and over my chin. I looked like a turtle with my head poking out of the vest—not a serious woman.

The reality of being shot was abstract, so I worked without the vest.

Bathroom breaks became a big deal again. Entering the new and improved lifeguard headquarters, I laid my gun belt on the floor of the stall, afraid to leave them unattended. Piece by piece, I peeled down—shorts, shirt, swimsuit. Somewhere under that uniform and all the gear, I was still a lifeguard.

I sat naked on the toilet and hoped no dispatch call would come. My brain played out a nightmare scenario: pulling everything on, a Carol Burnett moment, bursting out half-dressed, dragging my gun to a Code 3 emergency.

I started wearing a bikini, leaving me only half-naked if I had to sprint to an emergency. A two-piece was my scandalous secret in a generation when women lifeguards wore one-piece suits.

The swing shift was 4 p.m. to midnight, and every guard and ranger paired up for patrol. I became the unpopular kid at the junior high lunch table as partners paired up. I made it well known: I didn't want to wear a badge and gun, or the work that came with them.

I tinkered with my gear and pretended to look busy until, eventually, a lifeguard or ranger showed mercy and said, "C'mon, let's ride together."

Years before I arrived, ranger women like Paula Peterson, who entered the ranks in 1972, had already claimed this domain and firmly established themselves. But I wore a self-imposed scarlet letter on my uniform—a mark of my own disengagement. For the first time in my life, I didn't apply my assertive work ethic to learn and perform my new responsibilities.

Leo Miller was one of a few rangers who returned each summer during his break from teaching high school. I felt relieved when we worked together. Not much rattled him, and I watched closely as he kept his contacts low-key.

"Here you go," he kept things from escalating with the public, "let me help you put this in your car so you can get out before the gate is locked."

But even with Miller, the work could turn physical fast. One evening we responded to a drunk who insisted on trying to drive away. Like most drunks, the man flailed and slobbered, then turned combative. The three of us ended up wrestling on the asphalt.

I managed to get one cuff on, then the other—and heard Miller whisper calmly, "Debbie … you just handcuffed me to this guy."

I froze, then undid the damage. Miller laughed. And, decades later, he still laughs without making me the butt of the joke.

The lifeguards I'd worked with, now assigned to enforcement, had changed. They were rougher, with a mean streak: "You've got two minutes to follow my instructions, or you're going to jail."

*What a jerk* was always on the tip of my tongue as I watched these little boys with guns, my name for the lifeguards who thought law enforcement was all a game. They didn't care that these were real people's lives.

But instead of calling them out, I held my anger. I didn't serve as a role model to show them a better way. I wanted to be invisible and survive my shift without taking someone to jail.

Midway through my first summer working enforcement, something shifted. I started seeing ankle holsters and second weapons. Lifeguards assigned to enforcement winked at each other, pulled up their pant legs to show them off like a club handshake. Lifeguards began calling themselves "Sergeant" and "Captain," wearing bars on their shirts that weren't in our uniform specs. Their postures changed. I no longer saw the lifeguards I once knew—only cops, with no trace of salty skin.

I stayed quiet, walked with my head down, and looked at my watch every 15 minutes. I just wanted my shift to end without anyone getting hurt. My mind drifted to the moment I could take off the belt, feel warm water rinse my body, and climb into bed.

One late afternoon, I rode with Topar, who had helped

me when I got hit by the car. I felt comfortable with him. He didn't drive Code 3 for fun; no vehicle stops just to rack up tickets, and he knew this work wasn't a game.

We received a call to check on a woman close to our location. I exited the passenger side and followed Topar to a woman sitting on a blanket. It seemed as though she carried her life's belongings with her, within arm's reach of her body.

Quickly, something went wrong, and Topar yelled, "Put your hands where I can see them! Now!" She held her hands under the blanket and would not make them visible. I looked at him, and he pulled out his revolver and pointed it at her.

And in a split second, I had to back up my partner. I pulled out my gun and pointed it at her, too.

I was sick to my stomach. We were in a standoff with a woman surrounded by empty boxes of Cheerios, old clothes, and plastic bags filled with her life belongings. Time moved in slow motion, and we didn't look at each other, only forward at the woman. *How would this end?* I had no answer.

Bruce, our backup, a lifeguard and ex-Oxnard cop, walked through our gun sights and yelled, "Put your guns down." He reached under the blanket and pulled her hands out. The woman had a two-handed death grip on a hot dog.

We holstered our guns in silence. Shaking, I thanked Bruce. I needed a rock to crawl under and a trash can to throw up in.

I could have shot someone. There was no time for an ethical discussion. At that moment, I stood with my partner and tried to remember my training. If the hot dog had been a weapon, I would have fired.

My nightmares about missing a rescue now included taking a life.

Workouts helped me work through my stress. In the early mornings, I went to Belmont Plaza and swam miles. And, with a new pair of running shoes, I jogged miles, hoping for a runner's high. I'd been at Huntington for three years, and I was only 24.

Prepared for another shift, I had an hour free. I stood on shore, held my fins, and had time for a quick bodysurf. The waves were decent, and I swam outside. The first wave was fun, with a nice right shoulder. The surf was better than it looked from the beach. Ready for another wave, I started swimming back out when a strange unease hit me.

An uninvited thought entered my mind: *What else can I do besides lifeguarding?* I never imagined I'd even ask that question. But there it was, surfacing from somewhere I couldn't ignore.

One evening a few weeks later, I sat in the ready room and heard a gunshot. It was unmistakable and echoed in the Magnolia HQ.

"Ray's been shot," someone yelled.

It didn't make sense. I ran up the stairs to the second floor, and Ray sat with a bullet hole in his thigh.

There was little blood, and it looked like the bullet had gone straight through his leg. It smelled like burnt skin, with char marks around the hole. Ray snarled as he held his thigh.

There was a first-aid kit nearby, and I pulled out a couple

of 4x4 gauze pads and gently placed them on both sides of the wound. Soon the big first-aid kits appeared, and I moved aside to make room for the paramedics.

As Ray was carried downstairs to the waiting ambulance, Miller leaned into me and whispered, "He'd shot himself cleaning his gun."

*Poor guy.* But my empathy quickly gave way to my righteous and silent belief: *None of us has any business carrying weapons.*

Ray's accident was all hush, hush, giggle, giggle for a week. Then his self-inflicted shot fell into the category of old news. *No big deal. He just shot himself.*


The noises stayed with me. The screeching sound of cars on the Pacific Coast Highway, alongside the park, was familiar. But all too often it was followed by the crunch of metal on metal. My body absorbed a jolt, and a mental image of me on top of the car flashed through my mind—all too often.

Back on patrol with Miller one early evening, I heard the screeching, and then a crash. A call followed over the radio, "Respond to PCH at Brookhurst, multiple cars, and victims."

Miller and I were close by and drove Code 3. Outside the park, I saw a police car blocking the scene. Sirens filled the air. I ran to the closest car. The front hood was smashed and buckled, and I could see a woman in the driver's seat. In a fleeting and strange thought, I noticed her long, brown hair and red lipstick; she looked pretty.

We had no gloves or safety protocols, so I opened the passenger side of the car, crawled in, and told her, "I'm going to help you." She didn't respond.

The steering wheel had slammed into her chest, and my mind raced: Airway, Breathing, Compressions. *This isn't going to work.*

Below the steering wheel, her right leg was contorted at the knee, and there was blood, lots of blood. I needed something to stop the bleeding.

The driver's-side door opened, and I could see firefighters and medics.

"We have it from here," they announced.

"Right leg is barely hanging on," were my parting words.

I started to crawl backwards, out of the vehicle, covered in blood.

Between this life-and-death situation and the wreckage of the scene, I heard, "Nice ass."

A firefighter in full turnout gear thought that was the moment to comment on my butt.

*Fucking jerk. Prick.* I wanted to spit on him, but I didn't. I had no energy for him.

I remember the woman, and I remember what he said—his madness and stupidity aimed at both of us.

I don't know what happened to the woman. There were many accidents on PCH—some minor, many serious. Whenever I heard the metal-on-metal, I cringed and braced for the worst and did my best, hoping to hear the medics appear next to me, *"We have it from here."*

And when the noise, the injuries, and the anger added

up, and I began imagining my life without guarding—the phone rang.

Steve Long, my Pendleton boss and friend, asked, "Would you like to transfer back to San Clemente?"

My shoulders dropped, and I looked to the sky.

"How soon?"

Debra Trauntvein, Rincon 2008

12

## *Trained by Eddie*

Debra knew it wasn't a day to surf.

"The waves were gigantic, out of control, and I couldn't see the horizon. I decided to stay out of the water and paint pictures of waves."

She heard the lifeguards on their loudspeakers as they drove from Sunset to Pipeline to Waimea Bay: "Stay out of the water."

It was her first winter on the North Shore.

After graduating from Santa Barbara High School in 1972, Debra knew exactly where she would continue her education—Hawai'i. The location was the North Shore, O'ahu, and the subject was *surfing*. She arrived at her sister's little house in Kammieland with a surfboard under her right arm. "Patty, I'm home!"

The surf break next to their tiny bungalow was named

after a small general store, Kammie's, a beloved local spot for snacks, surf wax, and shave ice, located between Sunset and Rocky Point. Debra's goal was to surf, surf, and then surf some more.

She woke to the fragrance of plumeria and the earthy scent of wet red dirt—a world away from the sage and dry chaparral of Santa Barbara.

As she painted, her brush shook and her hand wobbled midstroke as a helicopter shook the frame of her tiny home. She grabbed her binoculars and stepped outside. The helicopter hovered above 35-foot waves. A Stokes litter swayed beneath, a rescuer clipped to the line.

"Cool," Debra thought. "I get to watch a training exercise."

But when a wave crested and knocked the rescuer off the line, Debra froze. *This is not supposed to happen.*

She held the binos tight to her face. The basket lowered again. This time it came up with the rescuer and a body, both pulled onboard the copter. Then it went down a second time, and then again. Three bodies.

Debra tracked the helicopter as it flew toward shore and landed in an empty field close to where she stood. She stayed out of the way but kept a close eye on the chopper doors as they opened. One after another, the three bodies were pulled out and laid gently on the grass. Debra rubbed her eyes. First disbelief. Then tears.

She was barely 18, and the ocean had always been a joy. But now it turned ugly. She looked again—three people drowned. Dead.

Two servicemen and one woman were swept into the surf at Waimea Bay. Maybe they didn't understand the lifeguards' warnings about the dangerous conditions, or they'd ventured out near the water while the guards were on another beach. The massive surf and fast-moving currents carried their bodies nearly two miles east to Kammieland.

The entire North Shore, a tight-knit community united around the ocean, was devastated. Debra was no exception.

Two years ago, Debra and I talked about the drownings. In her late 60s, she remembered the details with clarity, her words precise, like a witness giving testimony. But during a moment of silence, her voice wavered, and I saw the memory turn raw, something she'd carried all these years.

In the days that followed the drowning, Eddie Aikau gathered the young people along the coast, including Debra and her sister, Patty Irons. He led beach workouts, swam them across Waimea Bay, taught them how to read the ocean, and trained a new generation of lifeguards.

Eddie became a lifeguard on the North Shore in the early 1970s because he knew he could make a difference and save lives. After the triple drowning, he took action. There was no extra money, no "atta boy," just his deep and respectful relationship with people, his community, and the ocean.

Debra held the certificate that "hereby and therefore" awarded her lifeguard status. She looked back and said, "I became a lifeguard under the watchful eye of lifeguard Eddie Aikau."

She lifeguarded the Kuilima Resort Hotel and Country Club before it became Turtle Bay. She paddled out onto the flat lagoon and saw green sea turtles beneath her board, and warned people to stay off the reef, away from the dangerous breaking waves beyond.

During her time off, she ran into the warm, tropical water with her favorite surfboard, a 7'2" single-fin board without a leash. As she improved and grew strong, she surfed an 8' gun.

Board shapers, Aunties, and surfers soon to become famous lived a simple life on the North Shore.

"I surfed with legends before they became legends," Debra wrote about the early days on the North Shore. "I felt accepted by the community in and out of the water. I offered respect, and in return, they gave my sister and me advice—and our share of waves."

Debra stroked out at Sunset, or wherever the conditions were best for that day, and waved to Eddie in the lineup.

She surfed and lifeguarded until it was time to get on a plane and head back home to Santa Barbara.


The first thing Debra did upon returning to California was take a job as a pool lifeguard at an exclusive club in Montecito, where she guarded and cleaned up after the guests. Her priority remained to surf as much as possible.

After two seasons at the club, she walked into the Santa Barbara City Lifeguards Headquarters and introduced herself: "I'm Debra, and I'm interested in a lifeguard job."

The lifeguards hired Debra on the spot, impressed by her surf credentials.

She marveled at the young kids sprinting through the

sand and swimming through the surf. *Junior Lifeguards?* She'd never seen a program and immediately saw her future.

After her first summer as an instructor, the program's director stepped down, and Debra stepped up. For 19 summers, she led the Junior Lifeguard program, training both instructors and the next generation of guards. Girls and boys watched her every move. The JGs' days were full of buoy swims, jumping jacks, sand, and bodysurfing. The most important lesson Debra taught was to love the ocean.

And then, news from Hawai'i:

*In March 1978, Eddie Aikau was aboard the canoe Hōkūle'a, voyaging to Tahiti. When the canoe capsized near Moloka'i, he paddled out on his board to summon help. After the crew spent hours in the water, hanging on to the capsized canoe, they were rescued. Eddie never returned. His disappearance triggered the largest air-sea rescue in Hawaiian history, but his body remained lost to the ocean.*

"Eddie Would Go" became a rallying cry in surf and rescue cultures, synonymous with helping others, overcoming fear, and doing the right thing. In Hawaiian communities, it carried deep cultural honor.

Fifty years after Debra's first trip to O'ahu, we had a Zoom chat. She spoke with passion about the ocean. On the other side of the screen she wore her blond hair long, streaked with sun-bleached silver. As she shared her values with me about the ocean, I sensed that her true north was helping people—the most essential lesson Eddie had instilled in her.

She left lifeguarding years earlier and works as a caregiver—proud to say she is still saving lives.

Her words stayed with me; she carried Eddie's willingness to help, his gentle humility and leadership by example.

Debra offered no qualifiers between her various lifeguard jobs. Whether it was a calm pool, a quiet lagoon, or big surf, she never ranked one above the other—it was all guarding. I admired her quiet instincts and respect for the ocean. Nothing in her voice suggested she'd ever tried to prove herself to anyone.

"All I wanted to do was be in water," Debra smiled.


As I wrote this book, I had made a clear distinction: I was a woman "ocean" lifeguard. My bias oozed out in every line. I made rescues in surf, not flat water.

Lake Perris challenged my righteousness.

Perris was a man-made reservoir, a State Park in the Inland Empire of Southern California. When the heat hit—which was most of the summer—Perris was the place to go for more than a million visitors a year, to swim, boat, fish, camp, hike, and drink lots of alcohol.

In the 1970s, there were two main swim beaches: Perris Beach, with five lifeguard stands, and Moreno Beach, with four. The metal stands held a solitary chair with nowhere to move other than a ladder to go up and down. If a guard was lucky, there was a canopy for some protection from the sun.

But when the wind was up, the cover didn't work.

In the ocean, I had time to size up my water. I watched people arrive, checked out their swimsuits, how they approached the water, and whether they smiled or screamed when the first wave hit their bodies. These were clues that helped me get to a victim early or even prevent a rescue. I could offer options: "This is a dangerous area to swim. Let me show you a safer spot to have fun."

But at a lake? I'd never guarded a stretch of flat water with thousands of people and no way to know who could swim. How do you watch everyone at once?

One Perris guard remembered a 15-cent beach ball blown into the water. A visitor ran after it, and when he reached water over his head, he started to go under. Thankfully, a lifeguard was watching, reached him in time, and pulled the victim—and his prize ball—to shore.

At Lake Perris, there were years of up to six drownings. A seasonal guard might witness one or be involved in a CPR, while a beach lifeguard could work for years and never work a drowning.

Flat-water guards scanned right and hoped no one went down left, always watching for submerged bodies. Sometimes there was a panicked splash or a scream—if the guard was lucky. The alternative, the always-present possibility: one head in a mass of people disappearing without a clue, a subtle slide under the water.

Only later did I understand how hard it was for the Victoria Park pool guards in Gardena, where I'd learned to swim—a crowded, urban, packed pool.

I grew up in a generation still unsure whether women ocean lifeguards had the "right stuff." Women were accepted more quickly on lakes and in pools, maybe because that work was considered second-class. The same men who said women couldn't guard the surf didn't care as much who watched the flat water. What mattered was status—guarding the surf was what made you a "real" lifeguard.

There were crossovers. Lake guards became beach guards and vice versa. We rarely shared our stories. But beach guards, including me, thought we were special.

The myth of the ocean lifeguard remained strong. But decades later, I see it differently—the time we wasted judging instead of learning from each other. Lakes, beaches, rivers, reservoirs and pools alike demand respect.

Every body of water holds danger.

Erin Porter, one of the Pendleton women's posse, knew this better than most. She made my heart stop when she told me about a rescue at Doheny.

She was running relief, giving breaks, and ran past the San Juan Creek, which divided Doheny in half. When the water didn't reach the ocean, it formed a stagnant lagoon the guards called the "Polio Pit," an ode to the polluted water we endured but would rather not.

It was a breezy day, and the crowds were light.

Erin looked down along the edge of the creek and saw a set of hands—nothing else—reaching for the sky. Without thinking, she dropped her tube and fins, leapt into the water, grabbed the hands, and pulled out a child.

"She was about five," Erin said. "I looked square into her face and saw big, frightened eyes poking out behind long black hair, a wide-open mouth, and a scream that made no noise."

Erin held her tight to her chest and said, "We'll find your mom and dad." The girl, in tears, pointed to her parents, who were sitting a good distance away. They didn't realize she'd gone missing. They grabbed their daughter out of Erin's arms without a word and walked away in a huff.

We talked that night. Erin's voice softened. "If I hadn't been in the right place, she would have died." She paused, almost to herself. "A rescue is a good thing, right? Why did I feel so frightened?"

I never forgot Erin's story, or the child.


A few years ago, I was driving south from Santa Barbara on Highway 101. The ocean opened wide beside the road. As I passed Mondos, a clean, shoulder-high right peeled down the beach. I pulled over and stepped out of the car.

A woman on a single-fin longboard flew across the face of the wave, long blond hair with silver streaks streaming behind her. She arched her back, pushed her hips forward, and continued to milk the wave. I could feel her smile as she paddled out for more. Maybe she was Debra.

I watched until she disappeared into the lineup.

13

# *Home Again*

After Labor Day, it was time to exhale. The tourists washed the sand off their bodies, packed up their cars, and were quietly relieved to head home with sunburned shoulders. Kids dumped their inflatable toys, plastic buckets, and shovels into trash cans, and traded beach days for classrooms.

The 1984 Los Angeles Olympics were over, most seasonals were back at college, and the towers were shut tight until next spring. Cooler mornings hinted at fall, but the afternoons still warmed. Cirrus clouds drifted in from the south, and depending on the angle of the sun and the tint of my sunglasses, I saw soft purples, yellows, and silver in the sky.

I started my patrol down to the beach alone. *Was the trail always this narrow, the cliffs this steep and crumbling? Had San Clemente always been this beautiful?*

Parked in front of Tower 1, I took off my jacket and scanned the horizon. To my right, Catalina Island floated in the distance, its shape etched in my memory. At Huntington, Catalina sat closer, the view interrupted by the massive oil platforms Emma and Eva. What a difference thirty miles made. My heart was happy, beating slow and steady.

The tide was low, so I drove south toward Trestles—around Cottons Point, parked at Uppers and scanned the coastline. Surfers shared picture-perfect right-hand, waist-high waves. I imagined them in the lineup saying to each other, "Please, you take this one, I'll go next."

The water, of course, was glassy, and a couple of guys nodded hello as they walked past me, even happy to see a lifeguard on the beach.

I had run a short reel on repeat in my head about my return—dolphins, bodysurfing, friends. I'd romanticized my experience as a young guard at Pendleton, and believed I was returning to a lifeguard panacea, like Cheers, where everyone knew my name and hoisted a beer to me.

But there was a rumor going around the grapevine about me: "Debbie's changed."

The source? Nick. From the first day I worked Tower 1, when he drove me up the trail in his broad-brimmed straw hat, I wanted his approval and I still did.

I was 21 when I left. I'd been hit by a car and talked myself into carrying a gun I never wanted. I'd seen lifeguarding at its best and its worst. The rumor was true. Of course I'd changed.

Mike waited for me at the shop. He was still Bruiser—big shoulders, thick arms—but now at first sight, I saw a gentle man with a huge heart.

He gave me a grin and tossed his bowling bag of peace-officer gear into the unit, followed by his briefcase—the brains of our lifeguard operations.

"First," Mike raised his brows, "let's do a Yum-Yum run."

"Why don't you drive?" I suggested, not wanting to feel like his chauffeur to the donut shop.

There was another reason I wanted Mike in the driver's seat. Despite my years at Huntington and the experience I'd gained, I felt awkward, unsure of what to say, where to put my hands, and when to laugh. I needed time to figure out where I would land with my old crew.

Off-season lifeguarding came with a different set of job specs. No sprint-to-the-water rescues, just the steady work of maintaining readiness.

Physical-training breaks were an important part of my day. Depending on the conditions, I ran along the shoreline, paddled my new surfski from Australia, and swam to stay fit for the job. Still, I pinched myself. *I can't believe I get paid to do this.*

The most beautiful days were long patrols from the southern boundary of San Onofre, north to Boneyard at Doheny and the entrance to Dana Point Harbor—quiet days of careful watch.

Some mornings I traded the beach for classrooms. Local kids sat cross-legged, eyes wide at my uniform and rescue tube, laughing when I told them about peanut-butter-and-jellyfish sandwiches. I taught them how to spot a rip, why lifeguards carry fins, and tried to convince them to join Junior Lifeguards next summer.

The off-season also meant vacations. We put in our requests early for time off after Labor Day—Sierra backpacking trips and North Coast wine and abalone adventures in the fall, Baja surf trips and, if you saved enough money, big treks south of the equator, where it was still summer.

My favorite assignment was returning to Huntington each spring to teach lifeguard training. I parked my blue Toyota truck next to the Magnolia Street headquarters and jogged to the berm. From there I scanned from the Santa Ana River jetty to the Huntington Pier, picturing the towers filled with guards in the summer, the sand packed with tourists and locals shoulder to shoulder, and lifeguards ready to make thousands of rescues.

The classes remained young men, with a woman or two in each session. Rookies remained soaking wet, tired, and stinky, just like when I went through training. But I wanted the lesson planted from Day One as I stood in front of the class—women guards will be your bosses.

My favorite part of training was the last day, when we exchanged handshakes and I saw the pride as they carried their bodies with confidence. Even better? Packing up my truck and heading back to San Clemente.

Winter gave way to spring, and in a flash, it was the summer of 1985. The Fourth of July had come and gone. I was at Doheny HQ when Mike called me.

"Hey, Deb, look at the schedule, next Wednesday at San Clemente. See anything unusual?"

I ran my finger down the page and said, "Looks like a strong lineup."

Mike was quiet, so I looked again.

"With a couple of switches, I can move Sandy to relief, put Kim in the unit with you," Mike laughed. I felt him give me the elbow over the phone.

We became co-conspirators, and with a couple of erasers, a trade here and a move there, we made it so.


I was the early-morning unit at San Clemente. As the towers opened, I checked in with Tower 1, Kara Weber, a New Zealander, a black-sand Piha girl, who married a city guard.

"Nice waves, looks like a good day for a surf," she smiled, her surfboard propped up against the back of her tower. Kara was a steady guard, but at the same time, she grinned like she was guilty of something. She'd already smuggled a snake into New Zealand, a country famous for not having snakes. The gossip mill told me she thought I was too serious, and I think my silence told her she wasn't serious enough.

At Tower 3, Calafia Street, Mary's tower was open, and she waved as I drove by, making a silly salute to me from her deck in her red suit.

Kris, in Tower 4, waved me over. "It's going to be a busy day. Can you give me some extra water, and do you have any extra 4x4 gauze pads? You know what? Let me see what else you have in your first-aid kit." Pilfering a unit's first-aid kit was always a way to get an extra stash of supplies.

Finally, Tower 5. "Morning, Michelle."

This was one of her first days on the job. I remembered her from training as a strong swimmer, and I'd given her top points on my evaluation.

I gave her a thumbs up like DP used to give me. "Stay sharp. It's a beautiful day, and the surf is picking up. I'll make sure the relief guard gives you a good break."

Watching her from the unit, I remembered myself as a rookie—afraid and standing alone, not sure of myself and my responsibilities. Instead of driving away, I parked and climbed into her tower. It was so simple to stand with her and point out the things I was looking at and where action might develop.

Michelle relaxed and asked me, "Do we ever talk to the City Guards?" and pointed to the adjacent tower to her right.

I gave a sterile answer about backing each other up, but her question was fair. *We should check in with the City Guards more often.*

"Michelle, call and talk to me anytime about anything. We all have questions. Remember, okay?" I went back to my unit.

It was time to get back to Tower 1 and pick up my shotgun. Kim sat in the tower with Kara and gave me a big grin. She knew the plan. Once in the unit, she looked at me. "Everyone here?"

"Yes," I nodded as I watched Sandy walk through the tunnel, ready to run relief for the day.

It was an all-woman lifeguard crew on San Clemente State Beach. The towers, the unit, and the relief guard.

It was bright, sunny, and a swell promised rescues. Kim and I high-fived each other.

"This is so cool," she said.

Flash rips started popping at Tower 4, Riviera, and Kris had made six rescues within the first hour. Mary, at Calafia, was in and out of her tower, making safety contacts, warning beachgoers about the dangerous shore break. The day hummed nicely as Kim and I took a smug joy in being part of the all-woman team.

Off in the distance, rounding the San Clemente Pier, we all watched *Surfwatch* head toward us. Water peeled and sprayed off its big, beautiful, yellow bow. The operator and deckhand were still silhouettes off in the distance as its big twin diesel engines, totaling 900 horsepower, announced that the cavalry was en route—the men were coming to save the day.

Once *Surfwatch* was in State Beach water off Tower 5, I saw Captain Adam at the helm, with his deckhand, Larry.

On the sand, I supervised this beach. I coordinated responses, directed backup, and answered for everything that happened. But on that boat? I needed permission just to step aboard. I could never stay, never train, never be a deckhand—or aspire to be a captain.

Across agencies up and down the coast, rescue boat captains nodded to one another: "Women don't belong on rescue boats." There was no written policy. Boat operators simply had full authority to run their program as they pleased.

Captain Adam brought his own twist: he was a God-fearing man worried about visuals and the perils of being alone at sea with a female creature. From shore, rather than fixate on the injustice, Kim and I laughed at the idea that we could tempt him into sin somewhere between Dana Point and Seal Rock.

Erin loved to joke, "Don't worry, we're not pecker-peepers." We laughed again. But it was a sad laugh. Everyone knew: deckhands were hand-picked, and women were never picked.

Kim and I parked at Calafia Street, and I knew that Adam was counting: one woman, two, three, four, the unit, the relief guard—the entire beach run by "the females." Maybe it frazzled him or made him mad. I hoped so.

Why weren't women allowed as deckhands and operators? Take your pick. Strength was an oldie but goldie, a recycled excuse, disproven when women joined the ranks in the early '70s.

And engines, grease, and oil. "Women don't want to do this dirty work," was an assumption, not a question.

Rosie the Riveter, with her bandana and flexed arm, stood with six million other women who welded, operated cranes, and built ships and aircraft in World War II. And since then? Women kept showing up in oil fields, on factory floors, in labs, and in cockpits.

The excuses became flimsier over time. And yet the one that stuck—the one still trotted out with a straight face:

"Where will they go poop and pee?"

Deckhands and operators used a bucket or jumped in the water. "Turn around," they said and gave each other privacy. The question was a better obstacle when the answers stayed mysterious.

"Don't get your panties in a wad. We let you do everything else."

I didn't want to be a deckhand or a boat operator. Still, I was angry, my face red and my jaw locked, every time I saw the boat make its grand entrance. The message was clear: "Stay in your lane and don't ask for too much."

The work at hand put the injustice on the back burner, while Kim and I got a call from dispatch.

"4505, rescue Tower 5."

Kim and I saw the empty tower from a distance and drove with flashing lights to provide backup. Michelle was outside the surf in a good-sized rip, a victim wrapped in her tube. I climbed into the tower to watch the water, while Kim focused on Michelle and the rescue.

Michelle backstroked the victim to shore. The kid shivered and looked scared. A woman, who I assumed was his mom, ran up and grabbed the boy. She fell onto her knees, stroked his face, and pushed his hair aside. She took his hand and they walked away.

Michelle backpedaled to her tower, her eyes on the water. She was going to become a good guard.

As I returned to the unit, I saw Kim race into the water, no tube or fins. A thumping shorebreak wave slammed a toddler and crashed the child onto the sand. There was another wave coming in close behind. Kim looked like a superhero, flying, and with one big scoop raised the child over her head and straight into the air. Kim was body-slammed by the next wave and didn't budge an inch. She carried the limp child onto the dry sand.

I called dispatch and said, "Tower 5 rescue and first aid in progress. Hold for additional information."

A small crowd gathered around us, including the child's parents. Now alert, the toddler squirmed and cried, her face and body covered with sand.

Kim and I spoke quickly, looked at the small toddler, the force of the shorebreak, and told dispatch to call the paramedics. There was no way we could determine whether she had inhaled water or had any broken bones, including the possibility of a neck and back injury. Our equipment was not meant for a child this small.

Kim asked the crowd to move back, and I told the parents, "As a precaution, we called the paramedics. Help us keep her still and calm—she's going to be okay. We just want her checked out." I watched the panic on their faces as they held each other with one arm, the other on their child.

Dispatch radioed that medics were on the way, and soon after we heard sirens. Two paramedics appeared in firefighter gear, walking down the beach with a backboard and their big red trauma box. They checked the child's vitals, secured her on a backboard, and placed the board across the gear box at the rear of our unit. Standing on the back bumper, each medic held the board steady as we drove them off the sand toward the fire engine and waiting ambulance.

The afternoon slowed, and at 5 p.m., *Surfwatch* motored north, back to Dana Point to attend to special, mysterious, manly things.

Kim dropped me off at Tower 1, and I went off duty. Sandy jumped in the unit and worked with Kim until all the towers were shut tight. They drove a final pass on the beach, the sun low in the sky, and used the unit's PA system to notify the last beachgoers, "Lifeguard service is ending for the day."

The day with an all-woman lifeguard crew at San Clemente State Beach ended with 16 rescues, 56 safety contacts, eight first aids, and a bunch of missing kids and found parents.

The next day, there was an all-male lifeguard crew at San Clemente State Beach. No one said anything. No one ever did.

After work and throughout the summer, my apartment on Del Presidente was a gathering spot. Like Nick's house on a smaller scale, my friends knew my home was open most of the time.

Jerry volunteered to drive to Trader Joe's in Santa Ana and came back with bottles of Vinho Verde and Beaujolais. I smelled his treasured, soft, stinky cheeses the minute he arrived. He'd been spending his off-seasons in Italy doing art and had brought his new girlfriend, Sabina.

Kara showed up with her husband, Greg. A few others squeezed into my tiny place after hearing that pasta was on the menu.

Alex Peabody was a Santa Cruz guy who had transferred to Huntington Beach, and someone told him to head south and knock on my door. So he did—smiling, holding flowers and fresh thresher shark from the local Alpha Beta.

The hot water for the linguine hadn't come to a boil yet, but I was getting ready to slide the pasta in. Sabina grabbed my arm.

"No, no, no. Did you salt the water? We need to measure the servings." She pushed me aside and told me to chop some garlic, shaking her head at my attempt to cook.

Jerry put Bob Marley on the record player, and we rocked back and forth knowing everything was going to be all right. We kept pouring wine, grated parmesan on our pasta, and talked about travels.

Kara sat on Greg's lap, one moment making out with him, and the next, wrestling him to the ground. There was not a shy bone in her body. The neighbors started to bang on our wall.

I started washing dishes, and Alex came to help dry. It was obvious he'd learned good manners during his travels in New Zealand. The night was still young, and Jerry took Sabina's hand and said they were off to see if the moon was bright enough for a midnight surf at Trestles. Our little group scattered, bellies filled with good food and cheap wine.

I shut the door with my last visitor gone and looked at my new little sofa. There was a parting gift—a big red wine stain—a reminder that we were not yet completely tame.

San Clemente still took my breath away, and my friends made me feel valued and loved. The truth I carried now was that I had changed—we all had—and the change wouldn't stop.

14

# *Patty and the JGs*

It was 1974, and school was out for summer vacation. Kathy and her sister Patty sat at the kitchen table, eating big bowls of Rice Chex. They heard their mom from the back of the house. "Don't forget your towels. And peanut-butter sandwiches are on the counter."

Kathy was 10, a year older than Patty. They each wore white T-shirts with a big Junior Lifeguard logo silkscreened on the front. Underneath the shirts they wore one-piece nylon swimsuits with modesty panels, just like the other girl swimmers they knew.

They arrived at South Carlsbad State Beach at 9 a.m. and waved at their JG instructors, Mike and John—two smiling men in swim trunks with lifeguard patches, no shirts—who took charge of the group of 22 kids, half girls and half boys. A few JGs had white zinc smeared on their faces; most were already pink with the start of sunburns, and some would spend the entire summer with skin peeling off their noses. No water or hats; just brown-paper sacks with their lunches. They threw their towels in a big pile, happy to be in the sand, close to the ocean, and with their friends.

Kathy and Patty's dad, L.J. Richards, became a seasonal lifeguard in 1963 and continued to lifeguard every summer in addition to his job as a firefighter. When his daughters were old enough, he didn't ask them if they would like to join Junior Lifeguards. He announced, "You are going to do Junior Lifeguards."

Years later, I asked Kathy what it was like to have her father order her into the program. She didn't hesitate. "It was the best thing he ever did. It made me who I am today. I can adapt to anything."

He told us, "You can do it."

Kathy remembered her JG days with Patty, "We weren't afraid of anything."

On the beach at JGs, the sisters heard, "Settle down, everyone, let's get started." Lifeguard John gave the group a once-over look, no roll call or attendance sheets.

"Give yourselves some space. Remember the stretches we showed you."

The kids spread their arms wide and shoved each other playfully to make space. Age, boy, girl—it didn't matter in the sand. The JGs copied each other and looked up to the real guards in front of them. Rescue tubes and fins lay just off to the side. Arms moved in circles, and they bent down to touch their toes.

"Ok, now switch," they heard the deep voices of the men in front.

"Let's shake it up, I've got an award for the best Funky Chicken." John strutted, cocked his head back and forth, and flapped his arms beside his chest.

The group went nuts, circling and making clucking and chicken sounds, and begged, "Pick me, pick me!" The strutting slowed, and Lifeguard Mike put his hands around his mouth, as if he were holding a megaphone.

"You all win."

The children groaned. "That's not fair."

"Nice and loud now!" Mike launched into jumping jacks. "One! Two!" The children shouted the count back, voices loud and proud, all the way to 25.

The morning warmed, and next up was a run-swim-run. Patty loved anything in the water. Before the instructors even said "Go," she bolted forward, sprinted around the red cone, and dove into the surf. She lingered there, in no hurry to race to shore, throwing her body into the whitewater and diving under waves, until Lifeguard John waved her back. She ran out of the surf and skipped alongside him, smiling as they returned to the others.

Junior Lifeguard programs started as a way to teach young beachgoers about ocean safety, fitness, and environmental awareness—and it was a blast. Like soccer camp and Little League, Junior Lifeguards was a rite of passage.

"Are you signing Billy up for Capitola or Santa Cruz City?" a mom asked a friend in line at Safeway.

Each agency had its own twist, but the goals were the same: get kids moving, teach them about rips and beach safety, and ignite a connection with the ocean. Junior Lifeguard programs took root in the 1920s, when boys lined up in military-style formations behind guards in khaki uniforms. By the 1960s, JGs had exploded in popularity. Slowly, over the next decade and into the 1970s, girls were granted permission to join the programs.

At the Carlsbad JGs, during those first summers, Kathy and Patty didn't see any women instructors or lifeguards, but their dad told them again, "You can do it." They never thought otherwise.

At the end of a long day in the sun and surf, they dragged their tired, sandy bodies home, washed their feet off in the backyard, rummaged through the kitchen cupboards for some chips, and turned on the TV in the living room.

"Look, Kathy," Patty was already flat on the carpet. "It's *The Brady Bunch*!»

On JG sand and in the Brady house, boys and girls mixed easily enough. Beyond JGs, the picture was different. In 1974, only five women worked as ocean lifeguards in all of California. It would take two more years until the first woman lifeguard was allowed to work at Carlsbad State Beach.

As JGs chased after each other on the sand and in the water, a debate still raged—were women strong enough to be lifeguards? Years of discussion about women lifeguards dragged on in the men's ranks: "Where will they go to the bathroom? How many pull-ups can she do? Can the females handle the job when the shit hits the fan?"

Meanwhile the JG girls didn't even know there was a debate. They ran stride for stride in relays, touched buoys first in the surf, and claimed the front row in lectures, rapt as the guards spoke.

From my vantage now, 50 plus years later, it was so obvious—any attempt to stop these young girls was futile. Women and lifeguarding were already a done deal. You could see it in the girl who screamed the loudest in the morning exercise line, or the teenager who pretended not to hear when it was time to swim to shore; she needed to stay in the water to catch one last wave.

For Kathy, both JGs and lifeguarding were cherished parts of her life. For Patty, it became her life's work—the same girl who grew up in the ocean would devote the next four decades helping other children find that same home.

Patty shook her head and laughed, remembering her first days as a JG instructor—and the games she'd played as a young JG. She watched her instructors drag out a pole barely wide enough to sit on, balanced on two shaky sawhorses for JG pillow fights. As a teenager, she'd thought it was the best game on the beach—smashing each other over the head until only the victor remained on the pole, holding a pillow overhead. The loser lay on the sand laughing, waiting for another chance at battle.

Years later, as an instructor herself, Patty set up the pillow-fight arena, grinning at the memory. Before the participants even arrived, she put her hands on her head. *What am I thinking?* In a world of liability forms and accident reports, sending a child home with a concussion was no longer an option.

"Quick—hurry up." Patty and the other instructors tore apart the pillow-fight arena before the JGs could see it, the last trace of a different time.

"How many Junior Guards do you think you've trained?" I asked Patty during one of our recent talks. We tallied years, multiplied by participants, factored in different beaches, double sessions, and then gave up, laughing.

"Thousands? Ten thousand?" I guessed.

"Easily," Patty said with a nod.


Confession time. I was a JG Mommy. In the lifeguard world, that's the mom who helps with the program, runs errands, and sometimes hangs out on the beach a little too much. I didn't grow up in JGs, and as a guard I'd always watched the program from afar.

My firsthand exposure came when my children became Junior Lifeguards at Seacliff State Beach, in Santa Cruz County. Like a treasured T-ball card, I keep a photo of Ryan and Clare posing together, holding a rescue tube, wearing JG T-shirts, with Seacliff's pier and cement ship in the background. It's the picture I'd grab if my house was burning down.

It was the summer of 2003, the same year Patty was promoted to Junior Lifeguard Coordinator at South Carlsbad. Nearly 400 miles north, the Seacliff JGs were gathered in a circle, fidgeting and buzzing with excitement.

For one special day in every JG session, the kids swarmed their instructors: "Today, right?"

The energy built like Santa Ana winds—in Santa Cruz, we called them "hot offshores"—and static electricity filled the air. As if by osmosis, the RV-camper people parked farther down the beach seemed to know it was the big day. They carried chairs, "I Love My Grandma and Grandpa" mugs, and their dachshunds down to the sand. They established their territory and waited.

And then, Instructor Lindsey appeared. Her long blond hair was matted, with twigs hanging through it, looking as if it had never been combed. Her eyes were black, and red tears, maybe even blood, streaked down her face. She wore a torn, black, long-sleeved shirt with mismatched boots that came to her knees. On her right hand was a white-medical glove from the lifeguard first aid kit—sparkling just like Michael Jackson's.

There was no sign of Lindsey, the lifeguard, as we knew her. She bent her knees, raised her arms in a zombie pose, and Michael Jackson's *Thriller* blasted from speakers. She looked over the crowd of 100 JGs and lip-synced along while the kids screamed every word back at her.

The crowd, ages 6 to 17, lurched forward, their arms claw-ing, their voices shrieking as they transformed themselves into zombies. Lindsay had taught them the dance, and together, they became an MTV video. Parents and campers cheered, dogs barked, and the beach shook with laughter. People watching from the pier took pictures and applauded.

Lindsey danced like she was born for that moment, and the kids were all in. The more dramatic the better. She gave these JGs the freedom to be wild, a forever memory, and fun for the sake of fun.

And on Seacliff Beach that day, while we all experienced the magic that Junior Lifeguards can bring into our lives, at Station 1—the lifeguard communication center with a good stretch of beach visible miles in either direction—a guard sat watch over the JGs and all the visitors on the beach. A quiet guard was doing their job, so everyone else could enjoy theirs.

Back in Southern California, Patty had expanded the Carlsbad program to include Torrey Pines State Beach. Amy, a third-year JG at Torrey, loved to Boogie Board. It was free play, and she sprinted into the water with her board. She watched a peak roll in, turned toward shore, pressed her left hand down on the nose of the board, and kicked hard to catch the wave. Amy felt the momentum of the wave, grabbed the rail of the board with her right hand and laughed as she flew across the clear face of the wave. When it turned to whitewater, she turned out of the wave and went back out for another.

*I really want to learn how to do a 360 this summer.* She was determined.

On the way out for more waves, Amy saw a young boy struggling in a small rip current. Without hesitation, she paddled toward him.

"Hold my board," she told him, "I'll help you get to shore."

Amy looked around and decided to pull him toward the beach. She floated him on her foam board and let the whitewater hit her back so the boy wouldn't fall off. She watched a guard high-step toward them through the surf. The guard's rescue tube flew in the air, and she reached Amy quickly.

"I can take him from here. Good job." The guard looked Amy with a big grin. "You're going to make a great guard someday."

The instructors on shore stood with their tubes in the air, signaling the end of free time. Amy rode her Boogie Board through the whitewater to shore, ran to the group, looked up at the tower guard, and couldn't wait for that day.

Programs like this didn't happen by accident. They were built by people like Patty Richards, who understood that JGs was about more than teaching ocean safety. It was about creating a culture worth passing down.

When Patty had her own children, she didn't need to tell them, "You're going to do Junior Lifeguards." She listened to Katlin, Duke, and Mickey say, "When I become a JG…" The ocean was the Richards-Mackle family's playground.

They grew up bodysurfing, paddling, and sweeping sand out of the house every day.

"It was a tight community," Patty remembers. "We went to each other's weddings, birthdays, and celebrations. It was a wonderful way to raise a family. And now my children are lifeguarding with my friends' children."

Three generations of State Lifeguards in one family—L.J. Richards, then Patty and Kathy, followed by Katlin and Duke. Mickey took L.J.'s career path, becoming a paramedic firefighter. That's a lot of lifesaving under one family umbrella.

Three years ago, Patty finally signed her retirement papers. "I think I've given it my all, and it's time to pass the torch."

The JG instructors looked at Patty's big, empty shoes, a desk with pictures of her family, and thank-you notes from JGs covering the bulletin board.

"How do we replace Patty?" The guards shook their heads.

But Patty had a recommendation: her daughter. Katlin had grown up in Junior Lifeguards, was an instructor, and had been a lifeguard for 12 years. There was state bureaucracy to navigate; Patty couldn't anoint her successor. However, when the tests were taken and the interviews completed, the best candidate for the job was offered the position. Katlin became the new JG Coordinator at Carlsbad and Torrey Pines. It felt just right.

L.J. Richards had told his daughters, "You can do it." Fifty years later, Patty and her legacy of lifeguards had made sure an entire generation heard those same words.

15

# Kiwis

*Yanks*

There was a holy pilgrimage—a *Camino*—a once in a lifetime trip we were all expected to make. At Pendleton, the question wasn't *if* you'd go to New Zealand, it was *when*.

As a young guard in the late '70s, I listened to stories about big rescues on the beaches of San Clemente told in the same breath as rescues at Piha, the legendary surf beach on New Zealand's North Island—as if it were just a jog down the same stretch of sand.

The stories stretched even farther. I heard about surfskis I'd never seen and lifesaving contests in Maroochydore, Australia, where the victors were immortalized on the front of cereal boxes as national heroes.

Photos of guards and surf breaks from Baja to Bali filled guards' vans, the shop walls, and lifeguard headquarters. Maps with pins and circles marked far-off beaches and imagined destinations. Above the toilet in the maintenance bathroom sat a battered copy of *Lonely Planet New Zealand*, thumbed through by dreamers—hopefully with clean hands.

I'd only been on two flights in my life, to Texas and Hawai'i, both for swim meets. My other travels were through books. Steinbeck took me on the road with *Travels with Charley*, and Dervla Murphy pedaled me through Persia in *Full Tilt: Ireland to India with a Bicycle*. Their journeys felt real. I woke from sleep, thinking of Dervla, and wondered what saffron smelled like. But the truth was I hadn't been anywhere yet.

Now I was meeting lifeguards who had set foot on foreign soil and swam in different seas. I wanted to be like them. I was falling into the Pendleton guard life, on and beyond the beach. It was a rite of passage, a mark of worldliness, and I started planning my own journeys.

Carl, my lifeguard instructor-turned-mentor, stoked my travel dreams and told me about the Surf Club at Mangawhai Heads on New Zealand's North Island. "You'll stay with Paul, 'Whippet,' the president of the surf club," Carl said. "He likes to make sure the yanks are cared for and fed properly. It takes a while to get past his gruff exterior, but you'll love him—at least, his wife, Phillipa."

Carl talked about them like old friends I hadn't met yet, already waiting for me to arrive.

And while I waited to go to New Zealand, Kiwis came to me.

My second summer at San Clemente, Sharon Flavell, a lifesaver from Mangawhai climbed my ladder and joined me in my tower. She mesmerized me with her accent, wavy black hair, and pearly skin. I compared my arms to hers. She looked like she'd done heavy swim training, maybe even weights.

Her smile pulled my eyes off my water, and she spoke with an ease that made me feel like we'd known each other forever. She told me her family were dairy farmers from Mount Eden, Auckland. They spent their summer holidays at their "batch," their holiday home at Mangawhai Heads. "My whole family are lifesavers—my brothers and sisters, and my mum and dad."

Sharon told me about cyclones in the New Zealand summer, our winter. "The sandbar in front of the club can shift overnight, and the surf becomes huge and dangerous."

And again, I was told, "When you come to Mangawhai…"

Sharon wasn't just another exchange guard. Her mum, Marie, had been one of the first women lifesavers at Piha, and the Flavells would anchor the exchange for years to come.

Sharon's partner on the exchange, Shane Thorner, was also rotating through San Clemente. He was a guard from the black sands and rugged surf of New Zealand's west coast, Muriwai. Six-foot-five, he looked like he was raised on fresh milk and honey. I wanted to tap him on the shoulder just to see if he was real. *Stay cool, Debbie. He's just another guy.*

He grinned, looked out at the water, then back at me like he was up to something. The unit parked below us and pointed at the boat, and we sprinted into the water. I heard him laugh the entire swim out to *Surfwatch*.

Returning to shore, Shane was picked up by the unit and, for the rest of the day, given the VIP treatment, along with Sharon. We all wanted the New Zealand guards to go home and report that the San Clemente State Lifeguards were the best.


Carl organized the after-work activities for the exchange guards, and Olamendi's was on the menu.

We met at the Mexican restaurant on Pacific Coast Highway in Capistrano Beach and squeezed into the iconic red-vinyl booth that barely held eight of us. The Virgin of Guadalupe looked down on us from the wall, surrounded by serapes, sombreros, and bright splashes of color. I sighed. It was all so beautiful.

Chips and salsa hit the table, then pitchers of margaritas and red-and-gold cans of Tecate beer. I leaned over Sharon to coach her through the menu—Mexican food wasn't common in New Zealand—and we settled on enchiladas and beans while the waiter worked his way around the rest of the table.

The place was packed, the booth overflowing. Extra chairs were jammed in, a table was shoved against the booth, until 15 of us were crammed together, yelling across plates and pitchers. Then the mariachi band appeared at our table, blasting "Guantanamera." Trumpet, *guitarrón,* violin, and guitar music filled the room, played by men in black *traje de charro* suits with silver trim and wide sombreros.

I loved the silver adornments, but the musicians must have been boiling in those heavy suits. Sitting shoulder to shoulder with Sharon, watching her laugh at the music, I thought how alike we were in that moment, even though she was from half a world away.

One of the musicians put a sombrero on Shane's head, and our Kiwi climbed on the table to belt out a song he'd never heard.

By the time the food arrived, the table was a mess of chips, salsa, booze, and laughter. Getting to the bathroom meant crawling under the table through knees and spilled beer—a ridiculous feat we did for each other instead of emptying the booth.

Olamendi's let us stay for hours. When the check finally came, Carl snatched it up to tell each of us down to the penny what we owed.

Sharon and Shane went home with California rescue stories, tastes of Olamendi's, and bottles of salsa tucked into their bags.

## *Aotearoa*

And then it was my turn. In the winter of 1983 and 1984, I traveled 6,500 miles south of the equator to Aotearoa, Land of the Long White Cloud—New Zealand. I was picked to represent the California Surf Lifesaving Association as an exchange lifeguard.

As I came out of customs wearing a yellow Tugs Tavern Run-Swim-Run T-shirt—not my best shirt, but a badge of honor that I'd done the infamous race—Sue Donaldson, the Auckland Regional Lifeguard Programme boss, was waiting. She wore a red-and-yellow lifeguard sweatshirt, and long, sun-bleached hair. Her broad shoulders seemed made for paddling miles.

She waved, grabbed my bag, and marched us forward at high speed.

"Right, hope you had a good flight. Let's stop in at my house and have a wee cuppa, and then I'll tell you the plan."

This was a woman on a mission, not interested in my details about the food served on the plane. I followed her footsteps, dragging my jet-lagged body close behind.


Sue had grown up in Christchurch, on the South Island, where her father was an early member of the North Beach Surf Club, joining before World War II. All of her siblings followed into lifesaving, and Sue herself passed her Bronze Medallion, the test to qualify as a surf lifesaver, at just 14.

A world-class kayaker, she thrived once women were finally allowed to compete on surfskis. By the time she moved to the North Island, her reputation was well established. Sitting on the board of directors of Auckland Surf Lifesaving—surrounded by men—she fired off ideas about how to professionalize the system. Finally, the leadership stopped debating, promoted her, and said, "You do it."

"Right-o," Sue answered. And she did.

New Zealand, unlike California, has a century-old tradition of volunteer lifeguards, women and men, who served throughout the country. Farmers milked cows in the morning, then peeled off their overalls to reveal lifesaver togs underneath—ready to hit the surf club and pull swimmers from rips by afternoon.

In the peak seasons—school holidays and Christmas—the Auckland programme trains and hires paid professional lifeguards to work the beaches on weekdays. The surf-club members are trained and serve as volunteer lifesavers over weekends during the summertime.

By the time I arrived, in 1983, Sue had hired and evaluated all the paid lifeguards for 14 beaches on both the west and east coasts of the North Island. She organized my schedule and training as an exchange guard and made specific assignments, so I'd experience the variety of conditions her guards worked, from the wild Tasman Sea to the calmer Pacific. I'd never had a woman supervisor before. *I think I'm going to like this.*

I loved hearing a Kiwi accent again. It wasn't British, not Aussie—it was uniquely New Zealand. Proper, with a twang, and delivered like the punch line of a joke. "Abso-loot-ly, let's carry on."

We loaded ourselves and my gear into her car. She drove fast, *Sweet Dreams are Made of This*, blasting on the radio while she drove on the wrong side of the road. I pressed my foot against the floorboard, trying to brake. She parked with a jolt and led me down the driveway to her home in Takapuna, Auckland's North Shore. I was tired, my nerves frayed, and it was hard to concentrate on all the new sights coming at me full speed.

Sue opened her front door, and gentle sunlight filled her home. My body relaxed. She pointed out the kitchen window to Rangitoto Island. "We might go out there if we have time."

With a steaming cup of tea in hand, she spread out a map and pointed to the beaches I'd be assigned.

"By the end of the month, you'll be tested and return home with a Surf Bronze Medallion certificate and a few other things." Sue winked at me.

The first stop was Muriwai, the rugged, black-sand west coast beach about a one-hour drive from Auckland. Sue and I climbed the sand hills, and I stared at a foreign landscape. Wind and sand pelted my face, the air damp and salty. Big seas hammered the coastline, rips pulling so hard I cringed.

Sue pointed north. "Sixty kilometers of black-sand, all the way to Kaipara Harbor."

She leaned in and lowered her voice, "Here's the plan. There are three paid lifeguards on duty at the club right now. Walk down on the beach, past the surf club, beyond the flags. I want you to swim straight out, through the rip, to the end of that point."

I looked at the black bluff—jagged, sharp—and the big surf pounding into it. My stomach flip-flopped. I squeezed my fists against my chest. *I'm an American lifeguard. I can do this. But jeez, this looks sketchy.* I swallowed hard. "Can I bring my fins?"

We crept near the surf club like two Charlie's Angels minus the hairdos, and Sue continued the plot.

"That's the rip that runs along the headland, Ōtakamiro Point. It's a quiet day, and I want to test the guards on patrol to see if they're switched on and paying attention. When you're outside, turn around and struggle a bit. Make it look like you're in trouble."

We never faked rescues at home, but I was on her turf, so I followed her instructions.

The beach was empty. I walked, avoiding contact with the lifeguards, wearing my USA Lycra swimsuit, trying to keep it from riding up my butt, while holding my fins. The black sand sparkled as I made my way toward the surf, looking for the best place to enter the water.

I waded into the cold, choppy water, feeling Sue watch me. Hopefully, the guards were watching me, too. I dove through an inside wave and started swimming, letting the rip help pull me outside. I kicked hard, showing off some Yankee speed in the ocean.

Being alone in big surf on a new beach was unsettling, but I didn't have time to overthink. I followed Sue's instructions, and once I reached the headland, turned toward shore and pretended to climb the ladder, vertical, elbows clawing at the water. Like the stinky sea lions at Seal Rock in San Clemente, I put on my best drama-queen performance.

It must've been strange for the guards watching me: a strong swimmer, powering through the surf, only to turn suddenly into a victim.

Sue watched from the high berm as two guards sprinted to the inflatable rescue boat near the flagged swim area. I'd seen pictures of these IRBs—bright-orange inflatables about 12 feet long, with an outboard strapped to the back and two guards perched on the pontoons—but I'd never seen one in action.

I used an eggbeater kick to pop my body high in the water and watched the boat launch. The IRB punched through the first line of surf, the motor grinding like a chainsaw as it cleared whitewater and flew over bigger incoming waves. Within two minutes it had spun around me, and the deckhand leaned out to grab me. As instructed, I said, "Sue Donaldson said to say hello."

The gig was up, and the deckhand grabbed me under my arms and hauled me in the boat. "Bloody hell, get in here!"

And then I saw the operator, Shane, grinning at me. We remembered each other from his exchange trip to San Clemente.

Back on shore, Sue stood in front of my rescuers like a professor, asking questions about why they'd chosen the IRB rather than swim out with a tube. The men shivered and stood at attention, wearing only their Speedos. Sue kept her gaze steady on them; her hand moved to her chin. She dismissed them when her questions were answered.

Watching Sue, I thought about how many times I—and every woman I knew—had stood in front of men, dripping wet, body exposed, answering their questions. I kept my smile to myself as the men reported to Sue.

"There was no right or wrong answer," she told me. "I just wanted to hear their reasoning."

I'd be working with that crew for the next few days, sleeping in the bunkhouse, eating meat pies, and keeping swimmers between the flags and out of some of the biggest and wildest surf I'd ever seen.

On my first weekend at Muriwai, there was a surf lifesaving competition. The car park filled fast with IRBs on trailers, surfskis strapped to car roofs, and competitors wearing club T-shirts and team caps tied under their chins. Shane pointed at the schedule board and said, "You should enter the Ladies' Swim."

I wasn't a lady, and I didn't know any ladies, but I figured it out quickly. Women lifesavers had their own division for competition, unlike California, where there was one division—"Men"—and women were allowed to join if they dared.

I lined up in the black sand with other women, excited to compete. I was elbowed and shoved off the starting line, but I shoved and pushed back and fought my way forward. The starter's gun went off, and I hit the surf—the first all-women lifeguard race of my life.

I'd met Brenda earlier, a lifesaver from Muriwai, and right away I watched her take the lead, an alpha Kiwi. She was an animal in the water. I grabbed ankles and pulled myself forward, trying to catch up, but I couldn't quite reach her.

We turned the can, and I swam alongside her, stroking hard, blasting Queen in my head—*Another One Bites the Dust*. But Brenda kept the lead, a half-body ahead of me and not giving an inch. Once in the breaking waves, I tried to make my move, but she made hers. We ran up the beach in first and second place, with Brenda, the victorious lady, leading the way.

I fell in the sand, tired and out of breath. Brenda reached down, pulled me up, and threw her arm around my shoulders, "Bloody good go, mate."

*Maybe I can beat her in the paddle race.* I still had hope.

Swimming and competing against other women guards was electrifying. Pride filled my chest, and for once, in lifeguard competitions, I didn't feel like an anomaly or a token.

I belonged in this space—a place where women guards could race hard, get gritty, and feel the thrill of victory and the agony of defeat.

I wanted that in California, too.

Weekdays, I was back on patrol, and Sue had placed me at Piha, 20 kilometers south of Muriwai. Another big surf beach with good-sized beach attendance, thanks to its easy drive from Auckland. The north and south sides of Piha were divided in half by Lion Rock.

Sue had been keeping tabs on me and the other exchange guard as we shifted beaches. As I came out of the water after a body surf, she was waiting on the club deck.

"I've got a wee treat for you," she said. We walked to the Rothmans rescue helicopter, named after the cigarette company, on standby beside the Piha clubhouse.

"You're going for a little ride—if you're game." I climbed in beside her, covered my ears, and felt my face go pale.

The pilot sat in the driver's seat, or whatever it was called. Closest to me was a guy in a jumpsuit bracing himself against the open doorframe. Sue flashed me a grin, we lifted straight off and into the air without a runway.

"Those are the Waitākere Ranges!" she yelled as my world tilted. A blur of green slipped beneath us, the helicopter banked hard until the ocean horizon swung into view. We skimmed up and over Lion Rock and out to sea. The copter turned north toward Muriwai.

I was disoriented, constantly searching for the shoreline. Suddenly I was pulled to the open door, my legs jelly, staring down at the wind-chopped water. Everyone pointed at me.

I jumped. Or maybe I was pushed. Either way, I hit the water feet first, like a penguin, holding a fin in each hand. And just like that, I was safe again, swimming toward the Muriwai Surf Club. By the time I was on shore, I was a brave, fearless lifeguard.

"It was so much fun," I said to anyone interested. My terror tucked deep in my gut for private memories.

Showered and with a cuppa warming me up, a wiry, frenetic man barged into the club. "You've had enough of this black-sand shit. Time to go east."

Paul was the Club Captain from Mangawhai, on the east coast, a two-hour drive from Auckland. He showed up unannounced, ready to mess with Sue's carefully crafted exchange-guard schedule.

He didn't look like an important guy, but he ordered me to grab my gear. He made me feel nervous. He stood still but looked like he was moving. I kept trying to adjust my vision to get a hold on what I was seeing.

"You're Whippet, right?" I wanted to be sure this wild-eyed, frenetic man was the guy Carl had prepared me for.

"Yeah, that's me." His grin widened, now that the kidnapping was successful.

"We're off," he said, laughing as he launched into talk about San Clemente. "Did you bring the fins?"

He said it like a Mafia boss, as if my stash of Voit Duck Feet fins, which were impossible to find in New Zealand, were my ticket into his club.

"Yes," giving him a quick, nervous look over my shoulder at the back of the car.

"First, we're going to take a quick look at some birds." Paul revved the car's engine.

He drove to a car park on the bluff, jumped out without a word, and sprinted toward the point. I hesitated. *Do I lock the car? Leave my stuff?* Then I ran after him.

From a platform at the end of the bluff, I saw the surf club below, the rip where I'd faked my rescue along Ōtakamiro Point, and now something I hadn't noticed—a living mass of birds. Thousands of gannets jammed together, golden heads bobbing, snow-white bodies stacked on every ledge. Their yellow feet flashed as they skimmed the surf and banked back into impossible landings. The air was an off-key symphony of honks, and the stink of guano mixed with salty air and kelp.

Whippet spat toward the rocks. "Bloody Muriwai. They never showed you this? Typical west-coast guards."

He grinned, already halfway back to the car. "Right, you've seen the birds. Now let's get you to a real beach."


## Mangawhai

After miles of crushed-metal road, I was glad to get out of the car. Phillipa, Paul's wife, greeted me, "Kia ora, hello. Just ignore him." She looked over at Whippet.

She smelled like fresh bread, a tea towel was tucked into her jeans, and she wiped her hands. "Let's have a cuppa, shall we?"

She was calm, even soothing to me, compared with Whippet.

*How did these two get matched up?*

We sat at the small kitchen table overlooking the estuary while their toddler, Sveny, cruised around our feet.

She gathered him on her lap and smiled. "I grew up close to here, Wellsford, about 20 kilometers over the hills from here. I'm just a country girl, really. I draw up a few building plans now and then."

Before I finished my tea, Whippet dragged me back out the door. "Let's get to the club."

We walked down the hill to the beach and straight into the pages of a Far Side comic strip. I felt like I'd been there before, but I hadn't. The Mangawhai club sat at the back of the beach, above the high-tide lines, with two yellow-and-red flags marking the safe-swimming area.

In New Zealand, everyone grows up knowing to swim *between the flags*—the safest place in the water, where guards keep watch.

There were a couple of dozen people on the beach. December was high summer season for Mangawhai. Whippet bolted into the clubhouse while I walked through soft, pale sand and put my feet in the Pacific Ocean—an eastern shoreline, thousands of miles from the beaches of California and below the equator, facing the opposite horizon, but still the same mass of water.

To my left, a long beach stretched as far as I could see, backed by emerald-green hills where sheep grazed on cliffs that melted into the sand.

"Debbie, get up here," Whippet barked. I walked in mini circles, trying to keep my eye on the unknown waters behind me while staying compliant with the command. For anyone watching me from the club, I was every cliché at once—sun-bleached, blond, American, out of place. A ready-made punchline.

Rochelle Flavell greeted me. "Sharon told me you'd be coming through." Rochelle, with black hair like her sister, was one of the paid lifeguards for the season and, at 16, the youngest of the six Flavell children.

"Mum's expecting you for tea tonight. I'll come and get you from Paul and Phillipa's."

Rochelle stood on the clubhouse deck overseeing the beach in her yellow-and-red lifesaver uniform. I looked slightly right at the "head" part of Mangawhai Heads—a massive barnacle-shaped rock attached to a long reef of jagged rocks, towering over the harbour mouth and estuary on the other side. It was a natural landmark for boaters out at sea, marking the entrance into the harbour, and could be seen for miles along the coastal beaches and hills.

Directly in front of the club was "the Bar," a long, shifting sandbank, reshaped by every storm and swell, yet steady enough to make swimming dangerous. On some days when the conditions were just right, the tide, swell, and the cosmos aligned, the waves were world class—at least the world according to Mangawhai.

A few things became clear within the hour. Tea was tea, unless tea was dinner, and tonight, I was having dinner with the Flavell family. And, just like Carl had said back in San Clemente, I was staying with Whippet and Phillipa.

"You need to be looked after and fed properly. You don't want to stay in that rat hole of a surf club," Whippet sneered.

*And Paul was the captain of the surf club?*


The smell of lamb was the first thing that embraced me as I walked across the grass to the Flavells' home. Then Sharon came up from behind and grabbed me tight. "So glad you finally made it."

I looked at the big, brown house that stood on the section, much bigger than the small batches—summer homes—that lined the road to the beach.

"Wow," I said with my hands on my hips, looking at the house.

Sharon said, "Phillipa was the architect. My mum and dad wanted a house big enough for the entire clan—and lots of friends."

The names blurred as I met brothers, sisters, Rodger, their dad, and Marie, the matriarch of her family. It felt like a reunion with long-lost friends.

Each morning, Rochelle, Peter, the other paid guard, and I unlocked the club storage bin, set the flags, and laid out the rescue tubes. When it was my turn to swim, I ran into the warm water and floated on my back, then swam along shore, fish darting beside me in silver flashes.

"Maybe mullet or kahawai," Rochelle said when I described them.

Weekdays were quiet. We kept beachgoers swimming between the flags and off the bar. In between, we made each other cups of tea and took turns on the paddleboard.

"When you come to California…"I told Rochelle, planting the same seed that had been planted in me.

When my shift was over, I hiked the emerald-green hills and walked back on the beach collecting exotic seashells—forty years later, still piled by my front door.

Life was good in Mangawhai; fresh bottles of milk on the doorstep every morning, crayfish on the table, and cooked chooks served alongside lamb. It wasn't entirely paradise. Nescafé was considered coffee.

At night, there were BBQs and, once, a fancy-dress party—the San Clemente version of the Fifth of July. Lion Red cans of beer in every hand, except when Sharon offered a few of us lucky ones her "Specials"—gin, tonic, and a splash of Just Juice with a sprig of mint. We danced to the surf club's homegrown band, Pus Guts and the Spunk Rats, with Whippet on lead guitar and other clubbies on bass, drums, and keyboard. They played Rolling Stones and *Eagle Rock* by Daddy Cool, an Aussie band I'd never heard of, but quickly loved the song.

Sharon, her stage name Sheena, was the lead singer. Grabbing the microphone, she pulled it close to her face and sang, *Gimme Some Lovin'*. I was halfway around the world, surrounded by costumes, laughter, and loud music in a yard—it could have been Nick's house. *How were these two places so alike?*

One afternoon, after patrol, Sharon and I were plotting a trip to the Four Square—the only shop in Mangawhai—and I was excited by the thought of finding chocolate. Then Marie, her mum, appeared beside us.

"Let me take Debbie for a visit."

Marie and I hadn't spent any time together yet, and she walked me to the far side of the yard. We sat overlooking the estuary.

"If you look carefully at the sand hills just beyond, you'll see nesting oystercatchers—*tōrea*—black birds with white bellies and long, red bills. They fly in pairs this time of year, protecting their chicks."

I scanned the estuary and realized I hadn't spent much time looking at anything besides the surf. A sharp piping call carried over the flats, and I spotted two birds driving their bills into the mudflats below.

"Is that them?" I asked.

"Yeah, that's right." Marie stayed quiet for a few minutes and continued to watch the birds. She turned to me and broke the silence. "So now, Debbie, tell me about yourself."

She made direct, deep eye contact. I squirmed.

I looked back at the water and started peeling off my résumé: swimmer, lifeguard, proud member of the exchange.

"Debbie. Tell me about *you*." Marie leaned uncomfortably close.

I knew I was supposed to dig deep, say something profound—but my mind went blank. I laughed.

"Help me out here, Marie."

She grinned, and the moment softened. We walked back to the house and made tea. Sharon headed off to the shop without me, and Marie and I began to talk.

Marie was petite, the kind of woman you could lose in a crowd. But as I sat with her, taking in her quiet strength, I realized she was beautiful.

She told me she'd grown up in a lifesaving family, her father an original guard at Piha in the 1930s. In the 1950s, before rescue tubes and IRBs, she had been trained to use the belt and line—the rope-and-reel rescue standards of the time. Still, the Piha Club boasted that the rugged west coast was "the sea of men," and women were excluded. So, Marie went and joined the Milford Girls Club, a lifesaving team out of Auckland that had carved out a separate space for women.

"I was on a bus with a team going to Paekākāriki for

Nationals," she said, "and I saw this handsome young man. Love at first sight. That was Rodger, my husband."

We bantered back and forth as I spilled my guts—inner hopes, fears, my love life, and ideas for the future. Marie shared her own journey of becoming a licensed counselor while raising six children. She was my mom's age, yet she made me feel as though we were equals, talking about ocean life, joys, and struggles.

That afternoon marked the beginning of something unexpected—a bond that would stay with me long after leaving Mangawhai. It grew into a relationship that lasted decades. The Flavell family, especially Marie, taught me to look beyond a first glance, beyond a first assumption.

Over the next 50 years, and still today, the families of Mangawhai and the Pendleton Coast have stayed connected. There were marriages, kids, and now grandkids who cross oceans to share one another's lives.

And today, during difficult moments or times of uncertainty, a voice comes into my head: What would Marie do?

# 16

## *Always*

I waved. I always waved at the lifeguards, the way kids wave at firetrucks. It was 2025, a morning thick with fog at Seacliff State Beach. The lifeguard lifted a hand and gave me her palm back, probably happy I had Bernie on a leash, then rolled south toward Manresa.

She drove alone in a white truck with "LIFEGUARD" stamped on each side and the round California State Parks emblem on the doors, a brown bear in the center. A high-tech yellow-and-red rescue board was strapped to the roof. From the sand, I saw the navy-blue collar of her uniform shirt. The whole setup looked sharp and professional. Nothing like my days wrestling a 60-pound Hobie plank from the 1950s on and off a rusty jeep.

From that brief greeting, I knew more about her than she realized. And she knew nothing about me: I wore no lifeguard T-shirt, I was an anonymous woman, one in hundreds she passed daily. But if we had a few minutes together, I suspect I would have known one of her training instructors, her boss, maybe even that she'd guarded with one of my kids. We would have found common ground, even friendship, quickly.

I had questions for her—the same ones I'd asked the early women lifeguards I'd written about. What made you become a lifeguard? Tell me about some of your rescues. What are your plans for the future? And what is it like being a lifeguard—and a woman—in 2025?

But she was gone, just tire tracks in the sand, the truck shrinking in the distance. I did know that if there had been a rescue in front of us, she would have stripped to her suit, grabbed her fins and tube, and swam out in the surf, just as I had four decades ago.


Last summer, at the John Wayne Airport in Orange County, I waited for my flight home. I spotted a woman wearing a Taplin Relay lifeguard T-shirt. The Relays were a famous lifeguard competition. I eyed her for a bit, and with my flight delayed, went up to her and asked, "Did you ever compete in the race?"

That was it. We were off and running. Names and stories spilled out, and we knew many of the same people. She told me about her years guarding at Hermosa Beach for Los Angeles County, and said, "Let's get a coffee while we wait."

People hustled by, speakers announced flights, and we sat intent and eager to hear each other's stories. We both worked as lifeguards on busy beaches in Southern California during the 1970s and 1980s. We reached into our memories and nodded at each other.

"Were the locker rooms a big deal where you worked?" I asked.

Her eyes lit up. "What was San Onofre like to guard? I used to go on my days off to Surf Club. And Huntington? I heard it was intense."

"Last call for boarding." My flight number came over the speaker, and we hugged goodbye. She was headed to Seattle, and I had a short hop up the coast back to Santa Cruz.

I put my bag in the overhead compartment, squeezed into my seat, and settled in for the one-hour flight north. *I didn't even get her phone number.* We had so much more to share, and I assured myself I could track her down through the Los Angeles County Lifeguard network.

What I really wanted to do was tell her about my last rescue. As the engines roared and the plane lifted into the sky, I retold myself the story—my most difficult rescue.


It was springtime 2001, and I sat on the beach below my house at Platforms, part of Rio Del Mar State Beach. I'd made my home in Santa Cruz County, married the man who brought me flowers and fish—Alex, a career lifeguard.

My friend Sheila and I watched our daughters dig holes in the wet sand, all of us bundled up in sweatshirts on the cold, breezy day. I hadn't worked as a lifeguard for over 10 years.

Out of habit, I brought my fins to the beach. I always felt safer with them next to me. There was a notorious rip current at Platforms that pulled especially big and nasty in the spring, and as I looked to my left, it was getting bigger, pulling harder, by the minute.

On the beach with Sheila and our daughters, I scanned the water, back and forth, back and forth, as we chatted. I felt her pull—look at me while we talk.

But I couldn't. There was water to be watched.

Standing on a beach with a lifeguard, past or present, there was a dance ingrained in us. We stood side by side, faced forward, our eyes never meeting, while we scanned the water and chatted about the surf, the weather, our kids, or what was on sale at Costco. We knew there was water to watch, and that's what we did.

Sheila looked at me, and I looked at the water. Then I thought I saw something and looked again. Maybe 200 yards offshore, at the end of the rip, there was a head. On shore, a woman was jumping up and down, screaming.

*This was bad.*

I looked right, then left. No lifeguard unit. No tower. And no pay phone in the parking lot to call for help.

"Sheila, hold the kids."

I pulled off my sweatshirt and shirt, down to my jog bra and shorts, grabbed my fins, and ran toward the woman on the shoreline.

I entered the water and dove under the first wave. The water was brutally cold, and my head immediately began to pound. I pulled on my fins and couldn't see the head I'd spotted from shore.

I trusted the rip to take me outside the surf and swam hard. *Faster, faster*, I told myself. But that was it, I had no overdrive. I tried to kick harder, kept moving my arms, and screamed "Hang on!" to the victim I couldn't see.

Finally, a head, low in the water, not struggling. *Bad sign.* He could go down at any moment, slip under the water. I kept my head up, like a water-polo player, not wanting to lose sight of the victim.

"I'm almost there!" I kept screaming. "Look at me! I'm almost there!"

It felt like an eternity, but I reached him. I was scared and breathing hard. With no rescue tube, I grabbed him and tried to push my feet into his hips to make him float on his back.

"You're okay, everything's okay," I said to myself as much as to him. "I need to take a little rest and then I'll get us to shore, okay?"

*Take a little rest?* Who was this woman in my body? Certainly not a lifeguard.

I showed him my fins, as if they would give him confidence, but he started to panic. He was heavy—dead weight in the water. My idea was to get him to look outside and semi-float on his back. If he floated, I could hold an arm and shoulder and kick us to shore.

But he wanted none of that. He turned on his stomach and grabbed for my shoulders, like the struggling Marines at Calafia who tried to climb on top of me instead of letting me pull them to shore.

My body shivered. I needed a Plan B. "What's your name?"

"Hector."

"Okay, Hector, listen up!" I was shaking, but I yelled at him like a drill sergeant.

I pulled, kicked, and yelled our way out of the rip and into the surf zone. From there, I let the surf crash into us and used the waves and whitewater to push us to shore.

Finally, in the shallow water, I held him upright and walked, my legs shaking, to the dry sand. The woman on shore was his sister, and she thanked me. I saw no lifeguard units; there was no backup for this Code 3, emergency rescue.

I let go of Hector, unsure of what to do now that I had him on shore. There were no rescue cards to fill out, no one to check him out medically, and I needed to warm up immediately.

I walked slowly, my legs wobbly. I knew Hector would have died if I hadn't gone.

Sheila sat with our kids and smiled as I walked over. "Did you have fun bodysurfing?"

She thought I'd been out there having a good time.

From shore, a rescue can look like nothing. In the water, it can be the difference between life and death. I wasn't born a lifeguard with the skills to make a rescue. I had to learn to see what might be invisible to others.

Lifeguarding gave me perspective: a baseline that if everyone is breathing and no one is bleeding out, we can take a step back, lower the temperature, and give ourselves time to sort things out.

Writing this book, I met many women guards—all different. There was no single "female" story. We brought different bodies, personalities, experiences—and a shared passion to guard. We didn't want to be judged. We wanted to lifeguard.

Through lifeguarding's early decades, into the 1970s, men would drive by us, assuming women didn't have the right stuff. Guarding taught me not to make that same mistake—not to underestimate anyone standing before me.

Lifeguarding saved me. I became a better person. It taught me to see the world through the fragility of life, the strength of others, and the beauty of service. Lifeguarding gave me a path to become the woman I chose to be. Always.

# *Epilogue*

## *2025*

I stepped out of the hotel shower and straight into the bright lights of a full-length mirror. Naked, no place to hide, and the mirror offered no mercy. My 65-year-old breasts sagged, my belly bore proof of childbirth, and the deep wrinkles I'd learned to live with seemed sharper under the light. Sun damage had left its map of scars and blotches across my skin. My dermatologist called them "wisdom spots." I never laughed at that joke.

In an hour, I'd be walking into my past, the 75th Anniversary Celebration of State Park Lifeguards, three days of events at Huntington State Beach. I would see men who had last known me in my 20s, when we were all muscle, fearless, our bodies at the peak of our physicality. Now, years later, I wasn't sure how it would feel to be seen again.

I wrapped a towel around myself, leaned in close, squinted, and checked for any rogue chin hairs. Then I glanced at the dress lying on the bed. *Do I wear undies and risk panty lines?* I put on my New Zealand greenstone *toki*—the Māori symbol of strength—and let my fingers rest on its smooth surface, a quiet habit that brought me comfort over the years. Sue Donaldson had given it to Alex, and now it was mine to wear.

This wasn't 1978, running out the door with my fins.

George, Jamie, and I, old San Diego State friends, piled into Jeff's Sprinter Van, the 2025 version of a VW Van, and made the short drive to the event.

Jeff parked the behemoth of a car with great caution, and I wondered if any of us would show a small flicker of our wild sides that we shared long ago. We walked to the giant event pavilion on the beach, registered, and put on our name tags. Within two minutes, we'd lost each other in the crowd.

Pacific Coast Highway was still loud, and with only a small swell, there was no vibration under my feet, but I kept feeling for it. Quickly, I felt as if I'd never left.

I walked the gauntlet of people, just as Kim and I had done during our first lifeguard meeting at San Clemente. I looked at the person in front of me, their smile, a familiar voice, and, when that failed, a glance at the name tag. "Bret, I can't believe it's you."

And people came up to me. "Debbie, you look just the same." Or "Debbie Friedman, I wouldn't have recognized you at all!"

We fell into each other's arms and held on tight. In a microsecond, we remembered macro moments of life-altering events we had shared. A familiar name with an unfamiliar face held my hands, pulled me in close and said, "Remember the Bolsa shooting?"

And in that instant, the past wasn't history—it stood right in front of me.

The parade of long-lost friends continued. Many of us had lost touch, our lives pulled into jobs away from the beach, but in seconds, we reverted to our younger selves, our shared work, laughter, and life-and-death decisions during our most formative years.

We grabbed food and drinks while Longboard and the Knotty Knees, the headliner of the night, played their greatest hits. It was the '70s again, and I danced, thinking about how much I'd missed this energy.

I sat and looked at these friends, and I knew that despite my best efforts and promises, this might be the last time I saw many of them. One had gone on to become a NASA engineer. Another, a public defender in Arizona. And one had found her calling as a water-polo coach. My life in Aptos was quieter; I hadn't guarded in decades, but to most of them, I was still a lifeguard.

The evening wore down. We hugged and said our goodbyes. Then I saw a group of men squeezed together, their backs to me, in the far corner of the gathering.

"R-O, R-O, R-O-C-O! Rock Out, Rock Out, Rock Out with your Cock Out!" Voices cracking, they held each other tight.

I wanted to be mad, but they were so happy. I looked into the huddle, and two of them were holding hands. Like in their youth, they looked to the sky to thank their ROCO god. But this time, instead of thumping their chests, they just stood arm in arm. The group broke up; it was past their bedtimes, and they toddled off to get some sleep.

It was my bedtime, too. As I grabbed my purse, I felt a vibration in my feet that moved all the way to my chest. A south swell was building.

The next evening was the main show. We put on our cleanest clothes, pulled out our best manners, and posed for pictures. The Hyatt banquet room was filled to its max—families, old friends, and a new generation of lifeguards—a chance to share history and honor one another.

To my surprise, I heard my name called. I got up, my legs stiff, and felt a little numb as I received the Robert J. Isenor Award. I stood with lifeguards who had helped create the State Lifeguard program, looked at the other women on stage, all of us part of history. I was humbled.

Years later, I knew the most challenging days were not the rescues, but preventing them—staying alert and watching the water.

Lifeguarding wasn't Homer's *Odyssey*—not an epic test facing trials at sea or deciding whether to let women lifeguard. The real hero's journey was perseverance: staying prepared, watching the water, and keeping our charges safe. It meant being open to change, letting go of the fear of the unknown, and supporting one another.

There's a beauty in guarding: when someone's in trouble, we run without asking who they are, what they believe, or whether they approve of us. We just go. That same instinct is what we owe each other—to remember that our true strength has always been service.

On the final night, after food and more reminiscing, we gathered for storytelling. I sat on a panel with three other women: MaryAnn, a retired guard with a 30-year career; Calla, who worked for sixteen years in all aspects of lifeguarding, including training and the rescue boats; and Sandy, who built a Junior Lifeguard program that went on to change the lives of thousands of children—many of them went on to become guards themselves. I shared my own path, including the many women I met while writing this book.

We laughed about the awful swimsuits we wore in the early years, and we remembered the rules that kept us off the boats and out of units. The absurd and the cruel, side by side. And we remembered the men who worked hard to welcome and provide mentorship. It was clear as we spoke that there had been progress. But it was just as clear—there was more work left to do.

After the panel, the four of us felt a surge of energy. The chance to speak our stories out loud felt liberating, our experiences untold but universal, each different yet bound by the same themes. It was a common bond we hadn't fully shared before. I had done another panel like this once, and it carried the same feeling—finally speaking what had been left unsaid.

When the panel stories ended, the younger women lifeguards found us. They wanted to talk, ask questions, take pictures, and follow us on Instagram. They were the new generation of change. And it wouldn't stop with them.

What I've learned is that lifeguarding works best when we accept change, support each other, and remember our common goal—saving lives.

Back at the hotel, I put my feet up on the bed and pressed my *toki* against my chest. I wanted to reflect on all the things that had happened over the past few days.

But first, I needed to shut my eyes and feel the south swell.

# *Acknowledgments*

If I understood what it meant to write a book, I would not be holding GUARDED in my hands today. My friend Mike Silvestri once announced, "Those Pendleton guards—no one listens to them anymore, so they keep writing books." It rang true, and I followed in the footsteps of Mike Brousard, Ed Vodrazka, Nick Sopha—and a writing tradition that runs deep in our lifeguard community. I'm grateful you all gave me a path to move forward in happy ignorance.

My deepest thanks to Sarah Chauncey, my editor, for her smiles and steady encouragement as I found my voice and the story I wanted to tell.

I'm grateful to Jacqui Salmon, Amy Lynn Foster, and Mitch Gerber for their professional support in bringing the manuscript to publication.

Martina Nicholson, Jennifer Balboni, and my daughter, Clare Peabody—my first readers—thank you for your endless support and your ears as I talked way too much about the book I wanted to write. I could not have finished without you.

To my lifeguard community, every guard in this book, and the endless stream of guards who took my calls and shared their stories—thank you.

With gratitude to Diane Bridgeman for your encouragement and continued support.

To my family—my heart—Ryan, Clare, Alex Peabody, and Robley Levy.

# *Photo Credits*

Kim Raymont and Debbie Friedman
San Clemente, 1978

Dedication: Mike Brousard
Page 10: Tom Keck
Page 102: Courtesy of the Pendleton Coast Lifeguards
Page 129:
Top: Courtesy of Greg White
Middle & Bottom: Courtesy of Arthur Verge, Los Angeles County
Lifeguard Historian and LACO Lifeguards
Page 130:
Top: © Author Kai Weisser, Huntington Beach Lifeguards, used
with permission
Middle: Courtesy of the Pendleton Coast Lifeguards
Bottom: Courtesy of Ingrid Loos
Page 131:
Top: Courtesy of the Pendleton Coast Lifeguards
Middle: Courtesy of Bill Kramer
Bottom: Courtesy of Patty Richards-Mackle
Page 132:
Top: Courtesy of the Pendleton Coast Lifeguards
Middle: Tom Keck
Bottom: Courtesy of Calla Allison
Page 178: Jon Shafer
Page 248: Ed Vodrazka

# *About the Author*

Debbie Friedman was one of the first women hired as ocean lifeguards in California, beginning in 1978 at San Clemente and Huntington State Beaches. She shared her life with the late Alex Peabody, a career lifeguard. Their children, Ryan and Clare, grew up in Junior Lifeguards and worked as seasonal lifeguards. Debbie lives in Santa Cruz County, California, walks the beaches below her home in Aptos, and still watches the water. GUARDED is her first book.